bright ideas

professional lighting solutions for your home

Sharon McFarlane

RotoVision

bright ideas

A RotoVision Book

Published and distributed by
RotoVision SA
Route Suisse 9
CH-1295 Mies
Switzerland

RotoVision SA
Sales, Editorial &
Production Office
Sheridan House, 112/116A
Western Road
Hove BN3 1DD, UK

Tel: +44 (0)1273 72 72 68
Fax: +44 (0)1273 72 72 69
Email: sales@rotovision.com
Web: www.rotovision.com

10 9 8 7 6 5 4 3 2 1

ISBN: 2-88046-756-X

Editor: Leonie Taylor
Art Director: Luke Herriott
Design and Artwork:
Keith & Spike @ Absolute Zero°

Reprographics in Singapore:
ProVision Pte.
Tel: +65 6334 7720
Fax: +65 6334 7721

Printing and binding in China:
Midas Printing

bright ideas

professional lighting solutions for your home

Sharon McFarlane

contents

 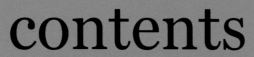

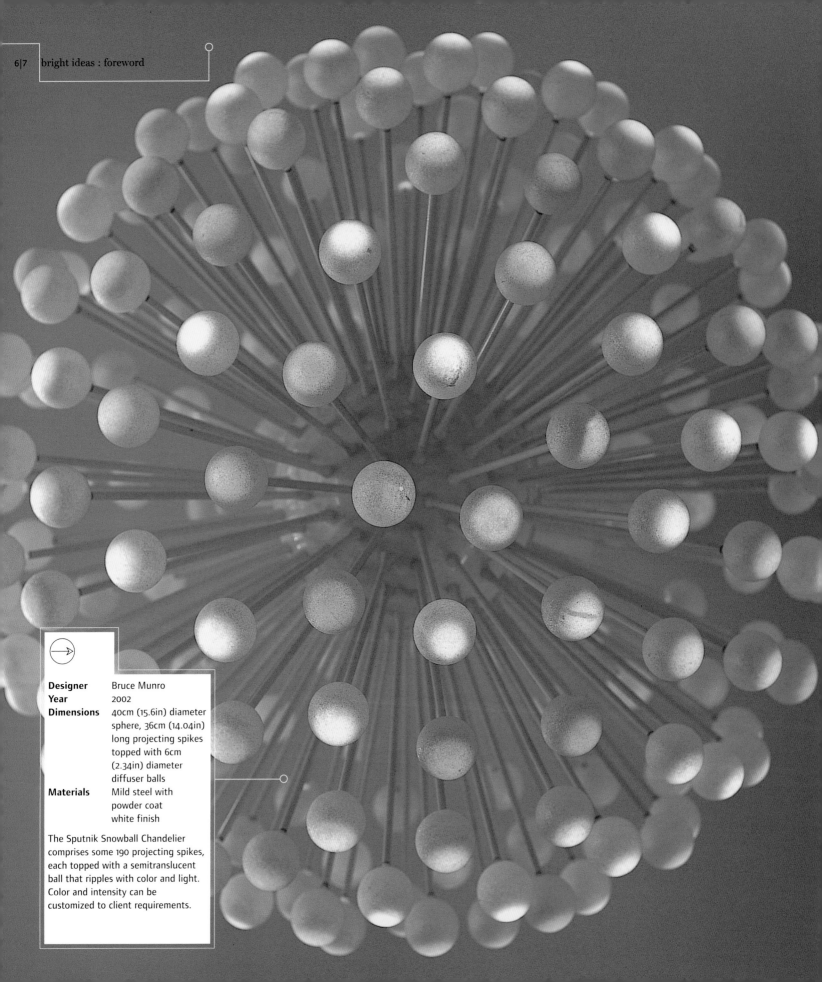

Designer	Bruce Munro
Year	2002
Dimensions	40cm (15.6in) diameter sphere, 36cm (14.04in) long projecting spikes topped with 6cm (2.34in) diameter diffuser balls
Materials	Mild steel with powder coat white finish

The Sputnik Snowball Chandelier comprises some 190 projecting spikes, each topped with a semitranslucent ball that ripples with color and light. Color and intensity can be customized to client requirements.

foreword

A good lighting scheme, in either a domestic or a commercial environment, requires a quality of emotion, backed by the correct use of proven and reliable technology—but never the other way around. A scheme should be about casting light on human emotion. These two thoughts are always at the front of my mind when designing a lighting scheme for a client, and they are the reasons for my enduring passion for light in all its forms. Good lighting sets moods and stirs emotions. It is an art in itself, but it must be used and seen in context.

My specialty lies in the design of handmade pieces—individually designed for a specific function, in a specific space, for a specific client. My sketchbook, never far from my side, is where it all starts. Tiny details in a house or in nature can be the inspiration for a luminaire. The shape of a leaf, the twist of a vase, a shell on the beach—they all end up in my sketchbook, from where the design process begins.

Good lighting works on subconscious emotion; it should not hit you in the face. This works up to a point—that point being when you wish to make a visual statement, which is where a chandelier or a luminaire comes into its own. For the past decade, designers have been tearing up the rulebook, developing chandeliers and lighting features with a radical, contemporary twist. Clients are realizing that such elaborate lighting statements are no longer the exclusive domain of the palace or stately home; they can also bring character to less traditional environments.

Introducing that quality of emotion, as well as fulfilling the brief, is the real skill of the lighting designer. Exactly how that is achieved is more difficult to define. But one can follow some hard-and-fast rules to apply in all schemes, and this book will give both the professional designer and keen amateur an insight into some of these rules.

"Rules are there to be broken," I hear you shout. I agree, and that is why it is so difficult to define a "good" lighting scheme—suffice to say that you will know it when you have designed one.

In a more general sense, good lighting can transform a space into one that provides the correct balance of functional and decorative light. The designer need not use fancy tricks or illusions, but must approach the design with honesty.

Designers and the public have realized what lighting can bring to both commercial and domestic environments, and this has led to a boom in the technological advancement of lighting. A good example of this is the rapid development of LEDs (Light Emitting Diodes), which will have a key role in the future of the lighting industry, in both residential and commercial settings. LEDs consume minimal amounts of power, are small and versatile, and have the added advantage that the light source emits virtually no heat.

This boom in technology should not restrict the designer's options when specifying a scheme—but it should be a valuable resource in his or her armory. More and more, the beauty of natural light, and all that it can bring to a space, is being appreciated. Rooms that are not blessed with large amounts of plate glass are being transformed by "piping" natural light into otherwise dark spaces.

Add this to the options of what so-called "intelligent" lighting can bring to a space—several different mood settings in any room, controlled digitally—and one begins to realize that we are merely scratching the surface of what lighting can achieve.

Bruce Munro, lighting luminary (see pages 106-107)

introduction

When Joseph Swann and Thomas Edison invented the first lightbulbs in the late 1800s, they did so with practical reasons in mind. Their driving force was to find a solution that meant that people didn't have to live and work only by candlelight when the sun went down. With such practical beginnings, it is perhaps unsurprising that for some time after Swann and Edison's invention, development tended to focus on lighting's functional role. New light fittings emerged, but few acknowledged the aesthetic, so the application of lighting in residential interiors tended to be less than inventive—a central ceiling light and a couple of table lamps being the mainstay of most homes.

Lighting may once have been the Cinderella of the home—the poorly dressed, utilitarian workhorse—but today Cinderella does go to the ball. The past few decades, in particular, have seen significant attitudinal changes as interior décor has become as much an expression of personal style as clothing is. Making a unique statement and injecting a sense of personality into our homes has become more feasible now that everyone can "Do It Themselves" with support from designers and retailers. We've come to appreciate that a good-looking interior is the sum of all its parts, and our choice of lighting is often considered as carefully as the rest of our furnishings.

While the consumer has an ever-increasing choice of retail or bespoke lighting options, unique aesthetic qualities are just as important as functional benefits—if not more so. Lighting designers and manufacturers, conscious of a more design-aware audience that is willing to invest in interior schemes where all the elements create a cohesive design, have responded with more sophisticated lighting solutions. Developments in lighting technology, in the light sources themselves, and in the materials from which fittings can be made, have given manufacturers and designers new tools with which to work. The result is lighting that can define a property—indoors and out—by altering mood and ambience as well as being functional. Lighting, ultimately, can become the soul of a home.

Bright Ideas will help you to design inspiring lighting schemes in your own home, showcasing the many types of lighting that can work to create atmosphere and mood, while also outlining new developments in lighting, such as the arrival of wirefree, portable solutions.

Each chapter takes a particular style of lighting as its central theme, featuring insightful comment from leading figures in the lighting and design industry, and setting out helpful tips to help you create the effects described. The book features case studies of both established international and emerging designers, whose work demonstrates the myriad stunning effects that can be achieved. The "Spotlight on" sections highlight commercial lighting schemes, including hotel, bar, and restaurant projects, to inspire domestic applications.

Prepare to be enlightened.

Architect	Altenheiner + Wilde
Year	1997
Location	Kayser private residence, Nauenrade, Germany
Photography	Thomas Mayer

Erco fittings were installed in the floor rather than the ceiling, bathing the entrance in ambient light.

modulations

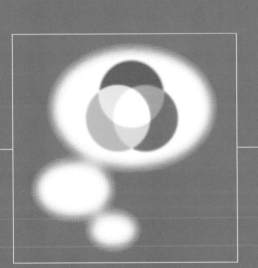

ambient

color

intelligent

Modulations:
Ambient

Ambient lighting is low-level lighting, so subtle by design that you tend to notice it only by its absence: atmospherically, an interior with effective ambient lighting extends an unparalleled welcoming feel.

Designers working on commercial projects such as bars and restaurants have long recognized the importance of ambient lighting in creating atmosphere, but the same cannot be said for domestic lighting designers. In the home, says lighting designer Bruce Munro, the idea of "using light to create atmosphere is still relatively new." Yet there are many opportunities for incorporating ambient light into residential schemes, which designers are increasingly exploiting. They have an ever-expanding number of tools to work with—including light sources and fittings created specifically with ambient lighting in mind—and they are starting to rise to the challenge of making innovative use of fittings, both revealed and hidden, to grace walls, ceilings, and floors.

The work showcased in this section comprises particular fittings designed to produce a more ambient level of light, as well as projects demonstrating how lighting designers have responded to ambient lighting briefs. Collectively, they demonstrate the striking difference that subtle atmospheric lighting can make to a room.➔

Designer	Focus Lighting, Inc.
Year	2001
Location	Private residence, New York, USA

In the hallway of this New York City property, it is hidden lighting, rather than the visible hanging pendant and chandelier, that gives the space a warm, inviting glow. That glow comes from a wall-washer hidden in the ceiling, while smaller artwork on the landing is lit via an accent fixture hidden behind a newel post.

The humble candle might have been rejected by Edison and Swann over a hundred years ago because of its ineffectiveness at providing a strong-enough level of light to live and work by, but it is a good starting point for understanding and appreciating ambient lighting in the home. Ambient lighting is not functional light that allows us to read, cook by, or perform other practical tasks—this type of lighting is, logically, called "task" lighting—but rather a softer level of light capable of setting mood or atmosphere.

When we want to create a more intimate dining experience, or a seductive bathtub mood, for example, many of us use candles to create a more contemplative atmosphere. Candles are an effective source of ambient light, but they do have their drawbacks. Melted wax can ruin surfaces in a home, and naked flames are a fire hazard. And as candles simply sit on surfaces—whether they are tables, shelves, or mantelpieces—they can't be used in the most creative of ways. Why not, then, replace these natural light sources—or at least complement them—with artificial lighting that can produce low levels of atmospheric light and that can be used in more inventive ways? That is precisely what many lighting designers are proposing today.

Lighting's ability to create atmosphere and make you feel more relaxed is a key reason why designers around the world are so passionate about working with the medium. For Paul Gregory, founder and president of New York-based Focus Lighting, Inc., installing lighting in a home is about much more than just adding light to dark spaces. He believes that ambient lighting has the power to elicit positive emotional responses: "Our goal when designing lighting is to make the individuals who will be in that space look and feel as wonderful as possible. When people are sitting in the warm sun in an Italian piazza, or on the beach during sunset, they look and feel really special. That is what we try to recreate with lighting."

James Sultan, senior lighting designer at Seattle-based lighting design consultancy Studio Lux, agrees that lighting has the capacity to make a homeowner feel more special, but says that this can't be achieved simply by filling a room with light: "Lighting designers edit the dark. It is just as important to plan for darker areas and/or shadowplay, as it is to illuminate a space brightly."→

Architects Altenheiner + Wilde
Year 1997
Location Kayser private residence, Nauenrade, Germany
Photography Thomas Mayer

Track lighting isn't something we would necessarily associate with bathrooms, but in this property such a solution was just right. A pendant-mounted track carries low-voltage spotlights from German manufacturer Erco (see pages 22–23).

Designer Focus Lighting, Inc.
Architect Karim Rashid
Year 2002
Location Morimoto Restaurant,
Philadelphia, USA
Photography David Joseph

In this restaurant, glass booths in the
seating area give a contrasting light
to that provided by the space's walls,
which seem to glow from within.
Using digital LED technology, the
partitions can shift from subtle tints
to vivid saturations of color. As the
color changes, so does the mood.

Ambient lighting, when carefully and subtly applied, can provide low levels of light to specific areas of a room without bathing the whole space in light. Thus, the play of light and dark that Sultan speaks of is achieved, to create a more atmospheric, welcoming form of light. Consider the effect of sitting at a candlelit table, with the way that light shines on the faces of the dinner guests while the rest of the room is in relative darkness—artificial ambient light can create a similar effect.

Certain light fittings are primed for use as sources of ambient light: wall-mounted fixtures, for instance. These are relatively simple to install and are available in a wide choice of shapes, sizes, and materials. Especially effective are those that wash light up or down a wall (commonly referred to as up- or downlighters, or wall-washers), and those that can throw a subtle degree of light up- or downward as well as across the wall surface. Obviously, it's important that these accommodate a low-wattage bulb—too bright a bulb will defeat the primary purpose of ambient lighting. When used in conjunction with a dimmer switch, the light level of such fittings can be reduced further, resulting in an even more intimate lighting experience.

The ceiling is also an ideal place to position ambient light. Think, for instance, of the way in which fiber optics can be used to create a "night sky" effect on a ceiling's surface, with each point of light replicating the twinkle of a single star. It's a wonderful look and, when used as the only light in the room, can make you feel as if you are relaxing under the stars. It is also possible to incorporate light into a ceiling cove or wrap it around the perimeter of the ceiling.

Cold-cathode lighting can be shaped to fit architectural features and thus follow the contours of a ceiling. It also offers an exceptionally long lamp-life—important when you consider how awkward it is to change lamps at ceiling level. Instead of a stark look, concealed trough lighting can give a moody feel. Using cold cathode in this way gives a room a subtle glow above, but with enough light to function.→

Distributor Blue Beacon Lighting
Year 2001
Dimensions Lightbox: H 12cm (4.68in), W 17cm (6.62in), D 14cm (5.46in)
Materials Aluminum

Blue Beacon's Fibre Optic Sparkling Star Kit comprises a fanless lightbox with 144 high-quality optical fibers, which, when installed in a ceiling, produces a starscape effect perfect for creating an ambient light in a child's bedroom. Of course, the effect could also be used in other parts of the home, such as hallways or living areas.

Designer Crescent Lighting
Year 1990–2002
Dimensions H 10cm (3.9in), W 10cm, D 3cm (1.17in)
Materials Aluminum, black synthetic rubber outer tubing

Combining LED technology with fiber optics is still quite a new concept, but as Crescent Lighting's LED Lightprojector System proves, the results can be stunning. The system comprises a sparkle-effect light projector with four white LED modules and connecting sleeves. The sparkle effect can be adjusted for each LED.

Applying ambient lighting in a residential interior is not limited to walls or ceilings, and the light sources that can be used to create ambient light are equally varied. A wide range of ambient lighting techniques is being incorporated into homes, and designers are coming up with new and inventive ways to approach the subject.

As in all design disciplines, however, design and functionality must be of equal importance. As lighting designer Bruce Munro says: "One must not forget about function." An effective lighting scheme is one in which direct, functional lighting works in harmony with hidden ambient lighting. It is crucial that residential lighting design makes use of a good mix of indirect and direct lighting and, furthermore, a balanced proportion of the two. It is also vital to combine functional with ambient lighting, to create different moods in different rooms while maintaining the functionality of those rooms. Using the kitchen as an example, you might want a lot of light on the cutting boards and cooking areas in the kitchen, and then more of a glow around the counter area.

Some lighting is capable of meeting both ambient and functional requirements. Uplighters and pendants are a case in point: pendants emit a warm glow, so they can be used as ambient lights, but clear, functional light shines downward from the opening in the bottom of the shades; uplighters, as illustrated right, emit an ambient glow through the material of the bodies, yet throw clear functional light upward.→

Designer   Diffuse
Year   2001
Dimensions H 14cm (5.46in),
               W 28cm (10.92in),
               D 13.5cm (05.27in)
Materials Ceramic

Uplighters, which, as their name suggests, are designed to direct light upward, are an ideal fitting for adding ambience to a room. When wall-mounted, as this porcelain uplighter shows, the area above is washed with light.

Designer   AJ Browne and Co
Year   2003
Location   Private residence,
                 London, UK
Photography Andrew Holt

Conscious that lighting is an essential ingredient in a kitchen, AJ Browne and Co came up with a solution that met both functional and aesthetic requirements. A fiber optic chandelier hangs above the dining area, with strip lights edging the ceiling. The most stunning feature is the glass floor, supplied by Arc Lighting. This is lit from beneath and creates the amazing feeling that you are floating. Coupled with the glass panels above the units, this energizes the room.

Accent lighting is a form of lighting that perfectly marries functional attributes with ambient atmospherics. Here, specific features in a room—an architectural or decorative feature, or a work of art, for example—are bathed in light, to give them prominence and highlight their importance. More often than not, the light comes via directional spotlights. When general, functional room lighting is dimmed or turned off to let the ambient lighting shine, accent lighting can help add to the atmosphere. Lighting a space is essentially a three-step process: first, consider the tasks that will occur there. Then, pick four or five important features in the room to highlight, whether they are columns, interesting wall surfaces, important artwork or bookcases. Ambient lighting completes the formula for an effective lighting scheme.

Designer	Piero De Marchis, De Marchis Sergison
Interior Designer	Silver Interiors
Year	2002
Location	Private residence, London, UK
Photography	Richard Seymour

While a fireplace is a great way of introducing natural light into a home, Piero De Marchis wanted to enhance this with hidden light that would provide an additional glow. The lighting effect is achieved with a flat-backed continuous ropelight set into the underside of the bench. This creates a comforting glow, and also serves as an excellent night light.

Spotlight on:
Erco

Erco is a leading manufacturer of light fittings, based in Ludenscheid, Germany. The company believes that all its luminaires should be used as tools for special applications.

Kayser House in Nauenrade, Germany, and Crescent House in Wiltshire, UK, are very different architecturally, but both properties use Erco fittings to achieve different ambient lighting effects. In Kayser's living space, the use of glazing allows a lot of natural light to spill in during the daytime. But when the sun goes down, Erco fittings wash the room in light. Track-mounted downlights provide general uniform lighting, while track-mounted spotlights direct lighting to particular features, such as a sculpture on the back wall. A back-lit glass-block wall acts as a room partition. There is also an integrated open fireplace.

Crescent House's architecture comprises two curved elements. One is used as the living area, and the other for sleeping. The two areas are separated by a curved corridor running the length of the building. In the living/dining area, ceiling-recessed wall-washers accentuate the wall as a space border that also serves as a reflector to radiate cosy, diffused lighting into the space. When it comes to lighting a table's surface — especially a dining table — pendants are generally the preferred solution. In this home, however, where the lighting needed to work cohesively with the architecture, a single integrated downlight creates the necessary light level and visual comfort.

The entrances to both homes also make use of ambient lighting. In Kayser, floor-recessed lights bathe the area in a warm light (traditionally, entrance lighting is positioned on the ceiling). Crescent's entrance features powerful, narrow-beam downlights that produce an illuminated "welcome mat" — a trick frequently adopted in retail installations.

Exterior lighting requires as much consideration as interior. The careful use of interior lighting in both properties has had a direct effect on how the homes are viewed from outside. The glass façade used within Crescent turns the house into a lantern at night. For the exterior of Kayser, the interior lighting theme was extended outside: downlight fittings used in the living area were also positioned in the front façade.

Architects Ken Shuttleworth, Foster & Partners
Year 1998
Location Crescent House, Wiltshire, UK
Photography Frieder Blickle

Ken Shuttleworth, partner at Foster & Partners, built this extraordinary country house for himself and his family. While being highly sculptural — both indoors and out — the simplified style of the building's architecture demanded a sensitive approach to the lighting used within it. Integrated lighting from Erco was used throughout. Illumination of walls is essential in a building of this nature. In comparison to vertical lighting, lighting positioned at wall level aids the perception of vertical planes, helps the orientation of visitors, and creates an impression of greater space. It was for such reasons that Ken used ceiling-recessed wall-washers in the house: they accentuate the walls, which also reflect the warm, soft lighting.

Highlights

○ Minimize clutter through integrally lit furniture.

○ Mix and match colors to alter moods.

○ Ensure that your lighting is continuous and compatible throughout the space.

Architects Altenheiner + Wilde
Year 1997
Location Kayser private residence, Nauenrade, Germany
Photography Thomas Mayer

For the exterior of this property, the architects continued the lighting concept used indoors. Two pendant downlights, the same as those used in the living area, were mounted in front of the façade, under the cantilever roof.

Architects Altenheiner + Wilde
Location Kayser private residence, Nauenrade, Germany
Year 1997
Photography Thomas Mayer

The exposed concrete construction of this house, alongside the three wings that had each been assigned a particular function—quietness, entertainment, and amenities— presented the architects with a challenging project to light. The living area contains an illuminated glass-block wall and an integrated open fireplace, dividing the living area and maximizing light levels.

Spotlight on:
Studio Lux

These projects exemplify how Seattle-based Studio Lux creates lighting schemes that seamlessly marry ambient, accent, and task lighting.

There are some rooms where we might assume that functional task lighting would take preference over ambient. However, when Studio Lux lit the kitchen area of the Highland Drive residence, it wanted functional and ambient lighting to work in harmony. While recognizing that a good level of light is a must for food preparation—achieved by downlights and under-cabinet task lighting—the firm wanted to blend this with the subtle illumination of pendant lights within the hanging pot rack.

When Studio Lux designed the lighting for the living room in the West Seattle residence featured, continuous fluorescent, dimmable strip lights, applied to the ceiling cove in the room create a generous degree of ambient light, balanced by downlighting. Lighting has even been applied to the fish tank, where red, white, and blue are mixed to achieve various effects.

The Mercer Island residence lobby is vast, neutrally decorated—an elegant space enhanced by appropriate lighting. Decorative wall sconces and a pendant chandelier are the most visible light fittings. These echo the styling of the space and provide different degrees of ambience. In addition, downlighters take the glare off the glossy tiled floor, while spotlights highlight the architectural columns. Such lighting continues to the back of the entrance area, where a matching chandelier hangs.

Highlights

○ Use ambient lighting to give a warm glow to kitchen areas.

○ Low-hanging ceiling pendants are great for bringing warm, ambient light to a dining area.

○ Dimmable strip lighting allows you to select a light level conducive to the mood.

Designer Studio Lux
Interior Designer Dorian Muncey
Year 1988
Location Private residence, Mercer Island, USA
Photography Dorian Muncey

The sensitive lighting here enhances the elegant and simple room design.

Designer Studio Lux
Architect Clint Pehrson
Year 2002
Location Highland Drive residence, Seattle, USA
Photography Stephen McGehee

The combined lighting here brings out the rich color and detail of the kitchen's vast horizontal surfaces.

Designer	Studio Lux
Architects	Olson Sundberg
	Kundig Allen
Year	2001
Location	Private residence,
	West Seattle, USA
Photography	Kim Carey

Strip lighting and downlighting combine to create a rich atmosphere.

Spotlight on:
Mark Humphrey

London-based interior and product designer Mark Humphrey was commissioned to design the entire interior scheme—both the furniture and the lighting—in this Georgian townhouse.

Humphrey applied careful lighting to the first room that one enters in the house—the main living area—while also making full use of the natural light that was available. Frosted glass was set in the wall between the living area and the washroom area beyond it (this is the wall with the shelf on it, to the right of the main picture). By day, natural light spills in from the washroom into the living area.

Humphrey placed lights behind the glass and mirror panels in the living area. Such lighting comes to life, naturally, in the evening, when it serves to create a moody and seductive atmosphere.

Various types of lighting were used in the kitchen area. Underneath the breakfast-bar area, lighting has been applied to the skirting plinth made of glass and cornice. This creates the effect of light appearing to spill from the underside of the kitchen unit. Elsewhere, a light cornice and spotlights were utilized.

Highlights

○ Maximize on natural light.

○ Combine glass and mirrors with light.

○ Place lights under skirting boards and cornices.

Designer Mark Humphrey
Year 2001
Location Georgian townhouse, London, UK

In the kitchen-bar area, the clever application of light to the skirting plinth allows light to spill from the underside of the bar unit and cornice.

Designer Mark Humphrey
Year 2001
Location Georgian townhouse, London, UK

In the main living area, the careful application of lighting works to create an open and spacious feel. Humphrey was also keen to make the most of natural light. A glass wall in the washroom lets such light spill into the living room.

Spotlight on:
Focus Lighting, Inc.

New York City-based Focus Lighting, Inc. designs lighting for leisure, retail, and residential environments. In many of its projects, ambient and accent lighting help create the mood and atmosphere that defines the space.

Focus's brief for Town Restaurant, situated within the Chambers Hotel in New York City, was simple: to create an intimate dining experience. The design of the underground restaurant, comprising three main elements—dining area, mezzanine level, and bar—presented the firm with several opportunities to create the desired intimacy.

The first element that grabs the attention of diners is a two-story wall, covered in square panels which appear to float away from the wall's surface and glow from within, thanks to the use of soft backlighting. The use of uplighting and subtle color filters creates an incandescent lightbox, giving a warm glow to the wood-veneer banquettes wrapped around the dining areas. To give the restaurant a more curvaceous look and to soften the corners of the space, Focus lit a series of hung crystal beads, to emphasize the "dazzle" effect. The tabletops are illuminated by track-mounted accent fixtures, hidden in ceiling coves.

In the mezzanine dining area, lighting is used to highlight decorative features: the plaster wall with its small, frosted square mirrors shimmers with subtle strip lighting, while the dark columns supporting the mezzanine are glazed with a wash of light.

In residential lighting schemes, Paul Gregory, founder and president of Focus Lighting, Inc., believes that light should seemingly be coming from sources such as a sconce, chandelier, or table lamp, while the light is in fact augmented with hidden downlights and adjustable accent lights. The hallway of a residence in New York embodies this philosophy. "The apparent source of light on the artwork is from the small hanging pendant. However, it is actually illuminated with a wall-washer hidden in the ceiling." It's a similar story in the living room, where chandeliers and sconces appear to illuminate the seating area, piano, and mantle, while in fact wall-washers and accents provide this illumination. Wall-washers also feature in the dining room to illuminate the dark walls and the artwork, and to provide an intimate and cosy atmosphere. Lighting behind the sheer curtains at the window creates another focal point.

Gregory summarizes his company's design philosophy: "Our goal is to make the individuals who will be in the space look and feel as wonderful as possible—as if they are sitting in the warm sun in an Italian piazza or on the beach during sunset."

Highlights

○ Hide subtle lighting around the room to augment main lighting fixtures.

○ Make your space multifunctional by adding lighting that can be altered to suit different tasks.

Designer Focus Lighting, Inc.
Year 2001
Location Private residence,
New York, USA

Lighting can make all the difference
between a home that's warm,
welcoming, and inviting and one that
has the opposite, negative affect. In
the living room, lighting helps create
an open, airy feeling, and, while the
chandelier above the chairs and
sconces on the mantle appear to
provide the glow illuminating the
seating area, specialty wall-washers
and accents provide the actual
illumination for the piano, mantle,
and seating area. In the dining room,
a cozy level of light is provided by
similar accent and wall-washers. The
study is, likewise, made more
welcoming through the incorporation
of shelf lighting to illuminate books,
wall-washers providing light on the
walls between the windows, and
lamps at either side of the couch for
task lighting.

Designer   Focus Lighting, Inc.
Architects   The Rockwell Group
Year   2001
Location   Town Restaurant,
                 Chambers Hotel,
                 New York, USA

When you're lighting an underground space, the challenge is to make that space as visually illuminating as possible. Focus Lighting, Inc.'s brief stipulated that the lighting also create an intimate dining experience. The grand walls glow from within, lit glass beads in the corner of the space transform empty corners, and lit panels directly behind the table are just some of the visual treats.

Trade secrets

→ "The best compliment anyone can pay you is initially not to notice the lighting but instead be wowed by the space in its entirety. When you're creating ambient light, don't be led by light fittings themselves. The space will dictate what you can use and what will work."
Bruce Munro *Lighting designer*

→ "The fundamental question should always be: what do you want the scene to look like? This leads to considerations not only of the activity but also of the most appropriate mood or aesthetic."
Mark Rowling *Erasmus Program*

"To create the best mood and ambience, lighting should be designed in layers—lighting the ceiling, walls (including art and architectural accents), and floor."
James Sultan *Studio Lux*

→ "Don't produce blanket-wash lighting schemes that do not allow for sensitive modulation of a space or the creation of a comfortable living atmosphere."
Henrietta Lynch *Fulcrum Consulting*

"An inventive approach allows one to alter the lighting levels according to the specific task or mode of the space."
Dave McCarroll *Kaplan Partners Architectural Lighting*

→ "Always include a dimming capacity, so as to vary ambient light to suit circumstances."
Phil Riley *The Light Lab*

Designer Catherine Le Teo
for Atelier Sedap
(distributed by
Optelma)
Year 1997
Dimensions Diam 35cm (13.65in),
D 10.8cm (4.21in)
Materials Plaster, matt white paint

French firm Atelier Sedap produces a
number of decorative elements for the
home—including lighting—all made
from plaster, a material traditionally
used to produce ornaments. Plaster's
unique ability to diffuse ambient light
is exemplified in this wall-mounted
piece. Bop is a circular fixture utilizing
a compact, energy-efficient,
fluorescent lamp. This emits a warm
glow from a central point, as well as
around the perimeter, where a halo
effect is produced.

Designer Kaplan Partners
Architectural Lighting
Year 2001
Location Strand Beach House,
Manhattan Beach,
USA

By day, natural light spills through
the glazed ceiling in this gallery area.
By night, wall sconces and spotlights
bathe the area in light.

Modulations:
Color

In the early 1990s, the buzzword in interior design was minimalism—crisp, clean, stark spaces, almost biblical in purity, but impractical for those with children, pets, or a love of red wine. The trend toward "maximalism," injecting vitality and personality into spaces, has reintroduced color as a key element in interior décor. Its addition to the home is an obvious way of personalizing a space and of making a strong visual statement. This can be achieved through furniture or paint, but also through lighting.

Lighting isn't about simply emitting "white light." It can incorporate colored light sources, or be diffused through transparent, colored materials to wash a room, from the wall, floor, or ceiling surface, or from within a piece of furniture. The choice of colored light fittings is growing all the time. Some emit only one color, but others offer the opportunity to create a subtle colored lightshow in a room, or bathe a space in various colors at different times of the day. Such lighting can have a considerable effect on the mood of a room, and is also thought to create positive emotional and even physical responses (see pages 36–37, 46–47).

Cross-fertilization between commercial, industrial, and residential design is becoming ever more evident. Hotels, restaurants, bars, stores, offices, and private residences are increasingly borrowing design ideas from each other. We see retail entrance areas that reflect lighting designs found in hotel lobbies; hotels and restaurants where lighting schemes are used to create a more homely feel; domestic bedrooms that are lit to create the same ambience as hotel rooms. The list goes on. This spread of ideas means that different strands of lighting are no longer the reserve of any one particular environment.

Colored lighting is a case in point. In theaters and nightclubs, colored lighting and color-changing lighting have long had a special role to play. In recent years, hotels and restaurants have also adopted the special qualities that colored light can bring to a space. Now, residential interiors are getting in on the act. We're not just talking about the addition of colored light to a home during the festive season or for parties—more sophisticated colored lighting solutions can add new dimensions to the home all year round.→

Designer	Tom Dixon
Manufacturer	Eurolounge
Year	1997
Dimensions	H 60cm^2 (23.4in^2)
Materials	Polyethylene

The Jack light's form was inspired by the child's game Jacks (hence the name). Available in red, blue, and white, it is described by its designer as a "sitting, stacking, lighting thing"—a comment that demonstrates the Jack light's variety of uses. It can be used as an illuminated seat; stacked up with other Jacks to create a glowing work of art, mixing to create a spectrum of colors; or, with a piece of glass or Perspex on top, makes a funky coffee table.

Adding a splash of color is a great way of enlivening our domestic spaces, making them feel more personal. It's also a surefire way of creating more visual interest in the home. But color, especially when it is incorporated into lighting, can have an even more powerful role to play—color therapists, or chromotherapists, assert that different colors affect human emotions, and thus have specific therapeutic benefits.

"Different colored light undoubtedly has an effect upon us," says Henrietta Lynch, head of the lighting department at Fulcrum Consulting, a multidisciplinary consulting firm that has worked alongside numerous high-profile architects and designers. Lynch adds: "We have evolved to deal and respond to colors in different ways. While there are relatively specific associations—for instance, red for passion—we also have physical reactions to certain colors. Our bodies respond slightly differently to colored lights in various conditions. At dusk, we experience what is known as the "Purkinje shift" effect, when our eyes become better able to see and respond to colors at the blue end of the spectrum."

James Sultan, senior designer at Seattle-based lighting design consultancy Studio Lux, also believes that colored lighting can reflect a current mood or help to change one's mood. He likens the effect of such lighting to music—a fitting analogy, as different types of music can elicit very different responses. When we want to relax, for instance, there's nothing better than classical music. Conversely, when we're getting ready for a party, we might choose more upbeat music. Lighting, especially colored lighting, can be used in a similar manner: some colors can create a calming effect, while others add drama and atmosphere.

Belgian lighting company Dark manufactures fittings that can be used to change color as well as light. Dark's director, Marnick Smessaert, says that his firm has become increasingly aware of how "colors can make people happy, express moods, can even change moods." Therefore, every fitting in his company's lighting range has its own choice of color to suit the emotion of the customer. Many of Dark's fittings can be turned into colored lights through the overlaying of transparent-colored materials, such as plastic. Colored gels, placed over a normal lightbulb, can also be used to create the same effect.→

Designer   Isometrix Lighting + Design
Year   2002
Location   Private residence, London, UK
Photography   Jamie Hughes

Isometrix's color-changing light product Colourwash (see pages 64–67) was initially installed within the lower living area of this property as the main light source within the space. The color theme was then extended to the en suite bathroom of the master bedroom. Within the living area, Colourwash was chosen to provide variable color to add heightened excitement. In the bathroom, however, the color is manually selected from one of the 256 colors available.

Colored lighting can be used to great effect in illuminated furniture, fusing standard light sources such as fluorescents with colored translucent resins, which become the "skin" for these pieces. LEDs, fiber optics, and cold cathode are further examples of how colored light can be achieved by combining material design with a normal white light source. The light source can be incorporated into the design's, so the lighting becomes part of the fabric of the building in which the furniture is placed, rather than being a separate entity.

London-based interior design and architecture practice Brinkworth also put cold cathode to good use when it designed a family home, although here the floor was lit rather than the ceiling. The practice created a "playroom" for the home's inhabitants—an empty space, devoid of furniture, that could be used as a space in which to relax, play, or entertain. Brinkworth's director, Kevin Brennan, explains: "We wanted to avoid ceiling lighting and wall lights that would bounce light off the polished plaster ceiling." They came up with the neat solution of introducing a lighting trough within the polished terrazzo floor to accommodate a color-flow lighting system, using three primary-colored cold-cathode tubes. These tubes are linked to a programmer that mixes color to the desired effect, allowing the client to render the room in any color for any event.→

Designer Dark
Year 2002
Location Decascoop cinema, Ghent, Belgium (part of the Kinepolis group)
Photography Point Studio

Belgian lighting company Dark installed color-changing lighting in this cinema. The result is lighting that subtly changes color every few minutes.

The possibility of having not just colored lighting but lighting that can change color has obvious benefits. One color might have the ability to tap into a specific mood, but having a choice of different colors means that a room can be washed in alternate shades to befit a range of moods and uses. Many designs on the market have built-in color-changing capabilities for this reason. It is playful and interesting to experiment with individual colors and combinations of colors. Unlike a preset color, having the control to set a precise color means you can change the feel of a room without reaching for the paint can. Traditionally, color is brought into the home via colored paint applied to the walls. This is fine for achieving a specific color, but, ultimately, a flat-colored wall is just that. You are stuck with that color day and night. Whereas a wall—and indeed a room—that is washed in colored light results in a more magical, visually stimulating, and mood-enhancing effect.→

Designer   Jeremy Lord, The
              Colour Light Co
Year   1999
Dimensions   Available in various
              lengths
Materials   Polycarbonate filter

Colour Wash is a programmable color-changing light system (see page 42). Jet (shown in use here at Deutsche Bank) is a stripped-down minimal-sized 3-tube version of Colour Wash, which is designed to be built into structures as a hidden light source.

Designer   Abbi Kiki, kiki UK
Year   2002
Location   Light Bar restaurant,
              Cambridge, UK

Kiki's client wanted red to be the predominant color in this interior décor scheme—something that could have ended up looking a little seedy. However, the soft red glow that emits from the hanging ceiling lights and that drizzles down the walls creates a look of pure sophistication.

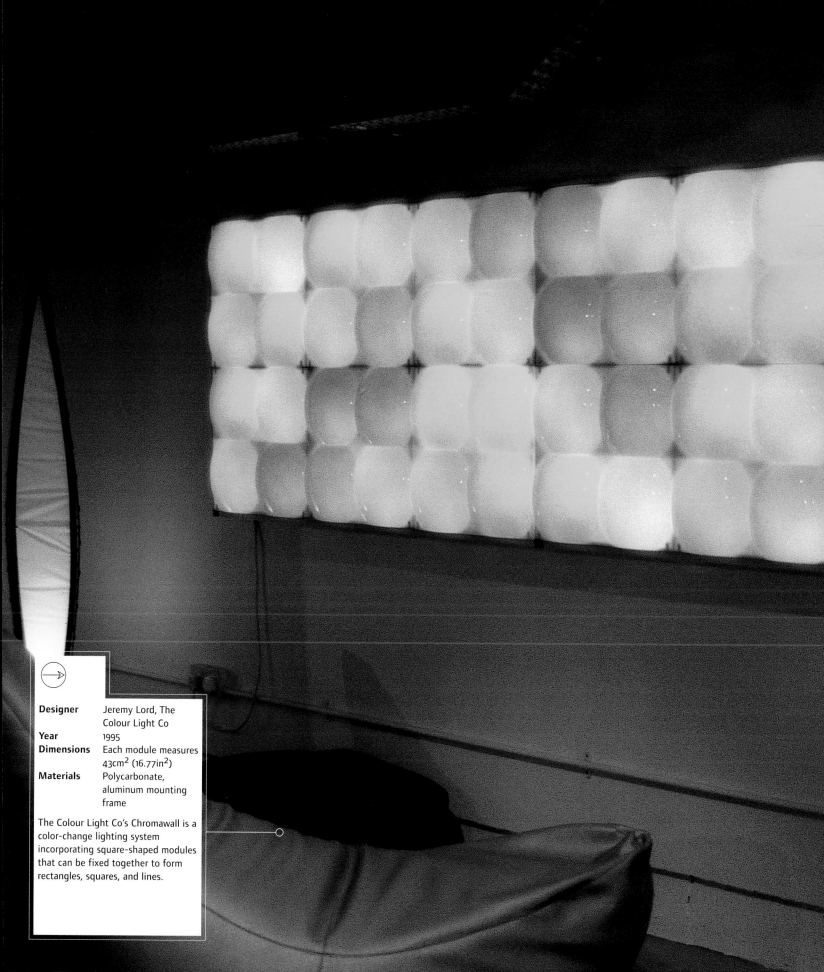

Designer	Jeremy Lord, The Colour Light Co
Year	1995
Dimensions	Each module measures 43cm^2 (16.77in^2)
Materials	Polycarbonate, aluminum mounting frame

The Colour Light Co's Chromawall is a color-change lighting system incorporating square-shaped modules that can be fixed together to form rectangles, squares, and lines.

Designer SHH Architects
Year 2002
Location Victoria Park Plaza
Hotel, London
Photography Francesca Yorke

A continually changing light show
now lights up the once dull tunnel.
Two rows of parallel filtered
spotlights have been inset into the
full 80m length of the ceiling.
Opposite the hotel entrance, a
vertical suspended wall was inserted,
made of 27 bespoke stainless steel
panels, leaning in at a gentle angle.
Some 20 buried lights, shining light
at different angles onto each panel of
the wall, dim and scroll at random.

Colored lighting, especially color-changing light, is a more sophisticated way of painting—it's a way of turning a space into an art lightbox. Lighting with colors is the most modern form of art, allowing you to "paint" moods with light.

Colored lighting can add a new dimension to domestic spaces, inside and out, and with so many different ways of incorporating such light, there is scope to be as imaginative as possible. Who doesn't like to see the magical presence of a rainbow in the sky? But rainbows, of course, are ephemeral, a momentary wonder. Colored light allows us to bring all the colors of the rainbow into our homes.

Designer	Focus Lighting, Inc.
Architect	Karim Rashid
Year	2002
Location	Morimoto restaurant, Philadelphia, USA
Photography	David Joseph

Cutting-edge architecture and design were the order of the day when Stephen Starr decided to open a second restaurant in Philadelphia. Architect Karim Rashid and New York lighting designers Focus Lighting, Inc. more than fulfilled this brief, bringing together their collective areas of expertise to produce a visual feast. Framing the restaurant are undulating walls lit from above and below, producing an ambient lighting effect wherein the walls appear to glow from within. Glass booths in the seating area provide a contrasting light. Using digital LED technology, the partitions can shift color from subtle white and pale tints to deep saturations of color such as pink, red, violet, and blue. As the color of the glass shifts, so the overall tone of the room changes.

Mood-creating colors

Colored and color-changing light can be more than merely decorative in interior lighting schemes: they can influence our sensory perceptions, emotions, behavior, and memory, as well as our physical and mental wellbeing. Color therapists—experts in chromotherapy—ascertain that the seven shades of the spectrum elicit the following emotional responses. (Full details for the designs shown here can be found on page 158.)

Red
Red is an invigorating, stimulating, warm, and energetic color, which can convey strength and vitality in an interior space. This color is particularly suitable for rooms used for socializing. Red is also reported to be a powerful healing agent for diseases of the blood and circulation, and can aid depression. However, it should be avoided by homeowners suffering from high blood pressure or anxiety.

Orange
This is deemed one of the best colors to use as an emotional stimulant, strengthening our appetite for life. An energetic color, orange is said to cheer the spirit and lessen irritability and hostility. Chromotherapists assert that orange can increase immunity and help with digestive ailments, but it is not a good color for those with a nervous disposition or who are easily agitated.

Yellow
Classed as the color of intellect, yellow promotes clarity of thought and stimulates the mind. The color of sunshine, yellow naturally lightens dull rooms or those not generally associated with happy thoughts, such as utility rooms. Yellow is thought to be helpful in curing skin disorders.

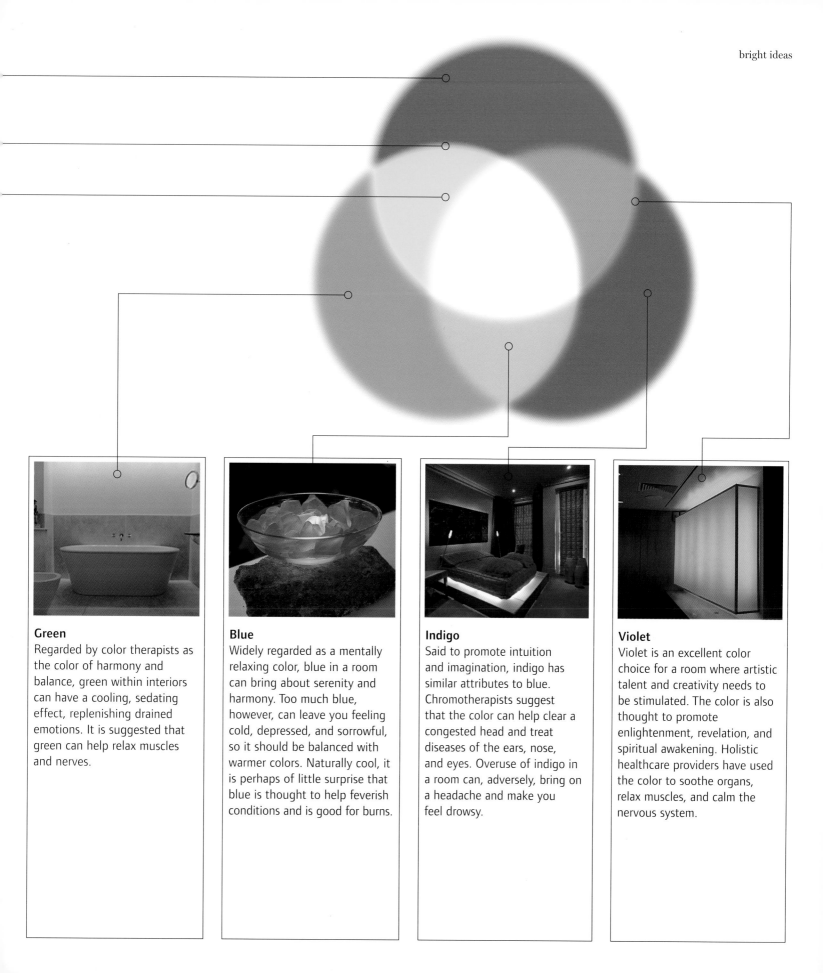

Green
Regarded by color therapists as the color of harmony and balance, green within interiors can have a cooling, sedating effect, replenishing drained emotions. It is suggested that green can help relax muscles and nerves.

Blue
Widely regarded as a mentally relaxing color, blue in a room can bring about serenity and harmony. Too much blue, however, can leave you feeling cold, depressed, and sorrowful, so it should be balanced with warmer colors. Naturally cool, it is perhaps of little surprise that blue is thought to help feverish conditions and is good for burns.

Indigo
Said to promote intuition and imagination, indigo has similar attributes to blue. Chromotherapists suggest that the color can help clear a congested head and treat diseases of the ears, nose, and eyes. Overuse of indigo in a room can, adversely, bring on a headache and make you feel drowsy.

Violet
Violet is an excellent color choice for a room where artistic talent and creativity needs to be stimulated. The color is also thought to promote enlightenment, revelation, and spiritual awakening. Holistic healthcare providers have used the color to soothe organs, relax muscles, and calm the nervous system.

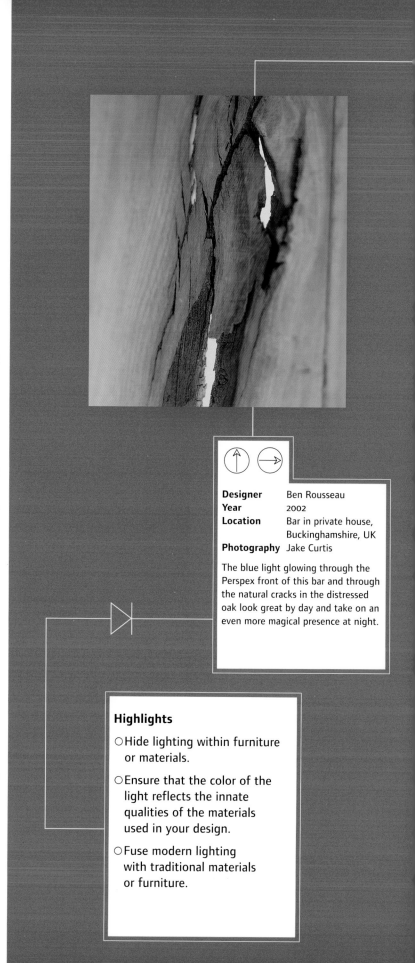

Spotlight on:
Ben Rousseau

British designer Ben Rousseau specializes in interior and furniture design where lighting is an integral element. In much of his work, he has utilized colored light as well as traditional white light. The bar design that Rousseau created for a client's home fuses a functional piece of furniture with colored light to stunning effect.

When Rousseau was first presented with the brief, the client had just laid reclaimed parquet oak floor with a glossy finish. Rousseau was asked to replace the existing bar area with a modern bar, shelving units, and a long sideboard, all made from a contrasting wood to the floor. Rousseau's carpenter, Jai Drew, chose distressed, untreated French oak as a perfect contrast to the glossy, immaculate floor.

Rousseau could have installed lighting around the bar to illuminate it, but instead chose to add lighting to the bar itself. It proved a clever way of "lifting" the wood and creating a more captivating effect. "I went for blue light because I didn't want the detail of the blue to be too dominant and I love the calmness of the color," explains Rousseau. "Also, I needed a color that would complement both woods. I could have used colored bulbs or Perspex with white bulbs, but the beauty of UV and live-edge blue Perspex was perfect for the job." By inserting blue Perspex in routered pockets, blue light bursts out through splits in the natural grain of the French oak that forms the side unit.

Rousseau continued the blue light theme elsewhere. In the main bar area, "it was concluded that instead of having the glow bursting through the cracks on the outside, I would pick the wood so that the cracks showed an obvious uniformity that did not allow the light to escape. Hidden light was reflected onto the blue Perspex, which was mounted over a layer of white Perspex to create a wall of blue color. The whole inside of the bar unit was covered in this way."

Sandblasted glass was applied to the top of the unit and to form the shelving. This complemented the Brazilian slate on the floor of the bar area, and details elsewhere in the room.

The design is a great example of what can be achieved when furniture forms and lighting—especially colored lighting—are fused. This project also shows how a traditional material—in this instance, wood—can be effectively combined with modern lighting techniques to create an innovative twist on standard design.

Designer Ben Rousseau
Year 2002
Location Bar in private house, Buckinghamshire, UK
Photography Jake Curtis

The blue light glowing through the Perspex front of this bar and through the natural cracks in the distressed oak look great by day and take on an even more magical presence at night.

Highlights

○ Hide lighting within furniture or materials.

○ Ensure that the color of the light reflects the innate qualities of the materials used in your design.

○ Fuse modern lighting with traditional materials or furniture.

Spotlight on:
Bushe Associates

British design practice Bushe Associates has established a reputation for creating innovative solutions for a variety of building types, including residential. This penthouse apartment shows how well-designed interior spaces can be enhanced by carefully considered lighting.

Working with Fulcrum Consulting's specialist lighting division, Bushe Associates' Tim Bushe explains: "We wanted to fuse indirect general lighting with accent lighting to highlight particular features and areas." The two firms decided that colored light would add visual interest and set the mood in many rooms: "To complement the neutral backdrop of the interior finishes, providing warmth or accent that could be changed to suit the owner's mood without altering the fabric of the building."

The colored lightshow begins as you enter the apartment — purple-fluorescent tubes line the inside of the cupboards along the entrance lobby that runs into the kitchen. These look striking against the gray cupboard doors and the zinc-clad screen opposite; the zinc absorbs the purple and is in turn transformed by it. In the bathroom, conceived as a stress-busting room, color-changing fiber-optic downlighters, linked to remote projectors, allow pivoting Perspex louvers and the steam shower enclosure to be washed in color.

In the living room and bedroom, a host of light fittings has been incorporated. While many emit traditional white light, color also has a presence. In the bedroom, a fiber-optic color-changing light source with a remote projector links in with the colored lighting in the master bathroom. In the living area, a surface-mounted color-changing uplight brings a wash of "moody" color into the space.

Conscious that lighting is as important for exteriors as interiors, Bushe Associates installed a number of light fittings in the apartment's roof terrace, including blue and white ground-recessed LEDs positioned under a timber bench. These, Bushe says, "provide a slightly alien, urban quality to the planting, since the garden is in the heart of a metropolis."

Bushe Associates wanted to ensure that wherever colored lighting was applied in this apartment, it would enhance rather than overpower spaces. This is why in many instances the colored light — particularly that from fluorescents — is concealed behind panels or lightboxes. The result is a dispersed, softer light that works in harmony with each room. Much of the colored light installed in this apartment is also energy-efficient.

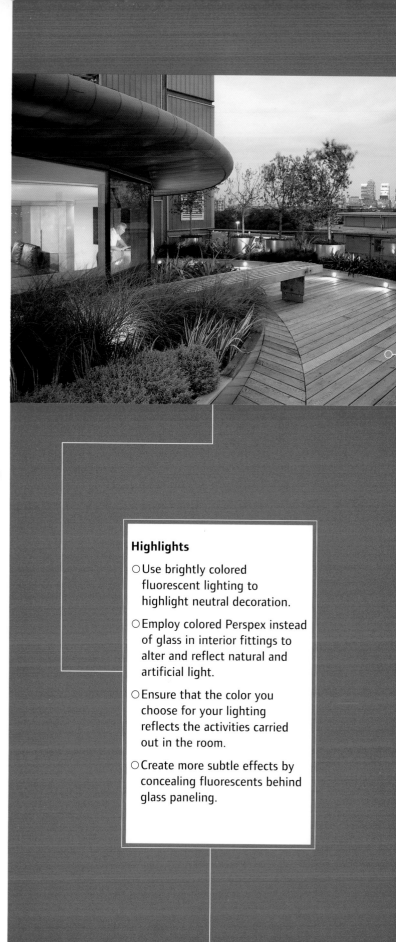

Highlights

○ Use brightly colored fluorescent lighting to highlight neutral decoration.

○ Employ colored Perspex instead of glass in interior fittings to alter and reflect natural and artificial light.

○ Ensure that the color you choose for your lighting reflects the activities carried out in the room.

○ Create more subtle effects by concealing fluorescents behind glass paneling.

Designer	Bushe Associates
Lighting Consultant	Fulcrum Consulting
Year	2002
Location	Cinnabar Wharf penthouse apartment, London, UK
Photography	Paul Tyagi/View

The careful application of lighting in the apartment's roof garden means that the owners can enjoy the space as much at night as by day. The underside of the timber bench is lit using LED blue and white ground-recessed fittings from Avanti, while wall-recessed fittings from Concord Marlin illuminate the dwarf wall. Mini Woody and Woody fittings from iGuzzini have been placed amongst the planting. Color is a key feature in the living room.

Trade secrets

Think about a palette you can live with. Use and mix your colors sensitively.

"Remember the effect color has on mood. Make colored lighting changeable if possible, using different tones to break up the space."
Phil Riley *The Light Lab*

 "Primary colors are often too stark. Instead, choose subtle hues, which are easier to live with and can enhance a space."
Nick Gant *BoBo Design*

"Don't use more than one or two vibrant colors for lighting. The two will only clash and compete with each other, and the whole effect will be ruined. Couple a subtle color, like off-white, with a vibrant color for contrast."
Thea Haddad *AJ Browne and Co*

"Every additional color reduces the impact of the others. It is a dramatic emphasis that is provided by the lights—excessive use quickly reduces the impact and degrades the experience."
Tim Bushe *Bushe Associates*

"Colored lighting can be used very effectively to enliven and dramatize the right space."
Henrietta Lynch *Fulcrum Consulting*

Lighting Designer   The Light Lab
Interior Designer   United Designers
Year   2002
Location   Millennium Hotel restaurant, London, UK

Working in collaboration with United Designers, The Light Lab linked a number of lightboxes together, each containing one yellow and one red fluorescent light. These are in turn connected to a Mirage scene processor that gradually increases the intensity of one color while decreasing the other. The effect is gradual and subtle—the whole process takes up to an hour—but has a surprisingly powerful, almost subliminal, effect on the ambience of the restaurant and bar below.

Designer Bushe Associates (in collaboration with The Unnatural Light Company)
Year 2001
Location Nordic Bar, London, UK
Photography Paul Tyagi/View

Take one design consultancy whose work has received many accolades in recent years, mix in the specialist lighting skills of a firm famed for playing with new materials and color in an adventurous way, and you have the ingredients for a very cool bar interior. Designed with a Scandinavian theme in keeping with the bar's name, Nordic's rustic interior acts as the perfect backdrop for some highly colorful and unique lighting solutions. Fixtures and fittings range from downlighters through to fluorescent lights. In the main, these are hidden from view, concealed behind lighting pelmets or recessed into soffits. Orange light makes a zingy injection of color into various elements of the bar. Elsewhere, The Unnatural Light Company has created bespoke lighting making use of dichroic film. When light is transmitted through this material, it takes on a multicolored hue, not unlike the Northern Lights—exactly what the bar's owners were after.

Modulations:
Intelligent

Lighting is all about facilitating a greater degree of interactivity with one's living space. Technology and design have progressed hand in hand so that the careful consideration we put into the lighting design of our homes can be pushed further by using fittings that react electronically to our lighting needs. Playful, responsive, and cleverly designed, this so-called "intelligent" lighting can take your space into the Space Age.

Intelligent lighting includes: fittings that can be adjusted to an alternative size; fittings that contain their own internal dimming system to control light levels; those that emit different colors; and, the zenith of intelligent lighting technology, the "home automation" system. Such high-tech, supersophisticated systems can control the lighting—and often other audio-visual and electronic equipment—in individual rooms or throughout an entire house.

Rather than relying on a simple light switch, which can turn a light only on or off, many intelligent light fittings have a control on the fitting itself in the form of a sleek dial or knob, or can be controlled via handheld remote controls. The same goes for whole-house lighting control systems, many of which also make use of sophisticated wall panels that act as central control hubs for a home's electronic activity.

The earliest form of intelligent lighting was the dimmer switch, which is still going strong. The first rudimentary dimmers were created for the theater world, where the possibility of dimming light levels was important for adding drama and atmosphere, and dimmers have since become a domestic lighting mainstay. Sometimes referred to as single-circuit controls, dimmers provide a simple and cost-effective way of controlling lighting in a room just by turning dials clockwise or anticlockwise. Dimmers are often found in dining rooms, where, as John Niebel, sales director at Pennsylvania-based Lutron Electronics, says: "Dimmer switches allow homeowners to dim the light to create an intimate dining atmosphere, turn the lights to full-beam to clean up, and set the perfect level for family dining."→

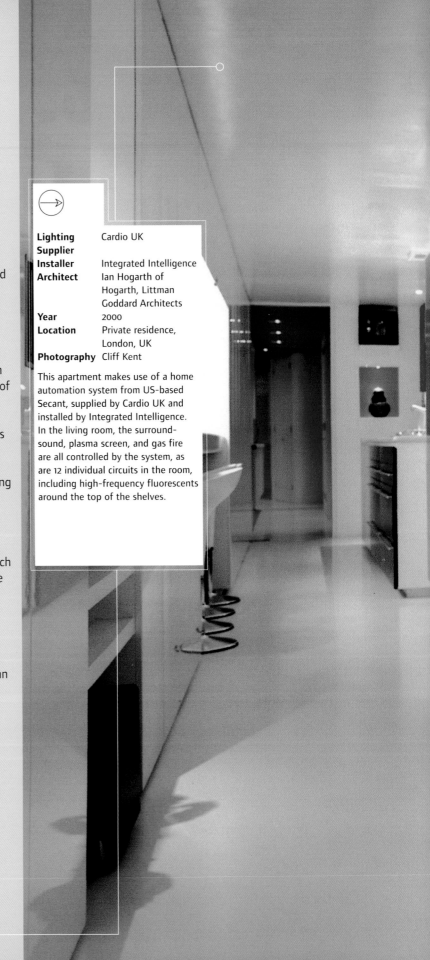

Lighting Supplier	Cardio UK
Installer	Integrated Intelligence
Architect	Ian Hogarth of Hogarth, Littman Goddard Architects
Year	2000
Location	Private residence, London, UK
Photography	Cliff Kent

This apartment makes use of a home automation system from US-based Secant, supplied by Cardio UK and installed by Integrated Intelligence. In the living room, the surround-sound, plasma screen, and gas fire are all controlled by the system, as are 12 individual circuits in the room, including high-frequency fluorescents around the top of the shelves.

Living areas can make use of a dimmer to vary the level of light emitted from a central ceiling fitting in order to create different moods. While living and dining rooms are ideal spaces to utilize dimmers, we have perhaps become a little stuck in our ways, not appreciating the number of spaces in which they can be used to great effect. This is a point that Niebel is keen to emphasize. "In a typical home, there are many other places where dimmers can be used to enhance your lifestyle," he asserts. He suggests the bathroom as one such place, where a dimmer would "eliminate that shocking blast of light at night, but allow you to enjoy bright light whenever you need it." The ability to control lighting in bedrooms can also be very helpful. In children's bedrooms, dimmers make great nightlights, easing a child's fears in the middle of the night, while dimmers in master bedrooms can create just the right comfortable atmosphere. Adjustable exterior lighting can also be very effective.

Most dimmers are designed for wall-mounting and are aimed at reducing or increasing light levels from the main source of light in a room—a central fitting such as a pendant, for instance. But it is not always necessary to have dimmer and fitting as separate entities. Many lighting manufacturers are creating fittings with integral dimmers—table and floor lamps, for example, which allow users to vary the level of light and therefore have far more control.

Dimmers, and light fittings incorporating dimmers, give you greater control over light levels in order to create mood or atmosphere. This can also be done through the use of intelligent lighting, which offers the possibility of controlling the type, or the color, of light emitted. We have already discussed the possibilities of colored light—colored light fittings, especially those capable of washing a room in different colors to reflect time and mood, are much more versatile than traditional white lights.

Color-changing light fittings, "Can create any color in light rather than paint, and consequently adapt to the change of seasons or to feelings, negating the need to repaint your room every time your mood changes," says Chris Miller, lighting projects manager and product designer at Isometrix Lighting + Design. His company's intelligent color-changing light product, Colourwash, is a linear lighting system that produces a saturated wash of colored light, controlled via a wall-mounted rotary unit or handheld controller. Users can either manually control the colored light show, or the fitting will automatically cycle through some 256 colours at a speed that the user can set—from slow to "disco" (see pages 64-65).→

Lighting	Isometrix Lighting +
Designer	Design
Designer	Ballast Projects
Architects	Watkins Gray
	International
Year	2003
Location	Beatrice Tate School,
	London, UK

Isometrix subscribes to the theory that colored light can be not only an exciting addition to an interior, but can also influence mood—a theory that it put into practice when it was commissioned to design a lighting scheme for the Beatrice Tate school, which provides education for children with physical and mental disabilities. The firm's Colourwash system (see pages 64–67) was used to light the school's multisensory studios.

Top
Without the effects of the Colourwash, the sensory room can feel cold and lifeless.

Right
By selecting warm, colored lighting, the space is brought to life.

Apart from its therapeutic attributes, color-changing light can be used to create a mesmerizing experience. It is, as lighting designer Jeremy Lord of The Colour Light Co says: "A great experience to watch different adjacent colors change—like listening to music. Sometimes it's almost an emotional experience, because you suddenly see a combination of colors that you really like (a bit like a musical chord) and then that moment has gone and you wonder if it will happen again. There is nothing like it in real life."

The musical analogy can be taken a step further. If controlling an individual light is like composing a melody, then how about creating an entire symphony—having control over a whole room's lighting, or, indeed, the lighting throughout a property? This is the height of intelligent lighting. Lutron Electronics, headquartered in Coopersburg, Pennsylvania, is recognized as one of the world's leading designers and manufacturers of such home automation systems. Entire-room controls, according to sales director John Niebel, generally work best in areas that typically have more than one lighting circuit in the same space, such as living rooms, dining rooms, kitchens, home cinemas, and master bedrooms. Entire-room controls can also be used in the garden, to manage different forms of landscape lighting. Ultimately, these systems are designed, Niebel explains: "To adjust several lighting circuits at the same time with the touch of a single button, allowing the individual to create lighting 'scenes' that are remembered by the control, and recalled by simply pressing a button on the dimmer. It's no different than recalling your favorite radio stations at the touch of a button, except in that in this case the lights will fade to the perfect lighting for entertaining, a family get-together, a dinner party, or for everyday use."

Whole-house control systems provide the ultimate in lighting control. While different home automation systems operate in their own unique way, the technology usually operates through the use of dimmers and switches that are networked throughout the home. Lutron's HomeWorks Interactive is an example of this: the dimmers and switches work independently most of the time, but can also be controlled from central areas within the home with wall-mounted or tabletop "master" controls. With whole-house lighting you don't have to adjust lighting to suit a particular mood. Scenes are set, remembered, and can then be recalled at the press of a button.→

Supplier	Bang & Olufsen Marbella SA
Installer	Leon Nafthaniel
Year	2001
Location	Private residence, Marbella, Spain

This house makes use of state-of-the-art lighting controls. Lutron's Grafik Eye system controls the lighting throughout the property, including the three bedrooms, dining room, and home theater. Using a remote control, the homeowner can create four different lighting "scenes" and an additional 12 scenes can be created via the system's master unit.

Lutron's Grafik Eye Bang and Olufsen series, as used in the Marbella residential property (shown on pages 58–59), is a version of the Grafik Eye home lighting control system that includes an interface linking all Bang and Olufsen electronic products for the home, including technologically advanced televisions, plasma screens, speakers, and DVD players. This means that not only the lighting but the home's audio-visual equipment can be controlled by one system, which can be operated from one simple remote control, the B&O Beo4.

One of the most impressive features of the system is its ability to adjust lighting levels automatically, depending on the level of natural light in each room. For instance, if the owner switches on his television at 8am on an overcast day, appropriate lighting will also come on. By contrast, if too much natural light is spilling in—which could have a detrimental effect on the room's fine art and furniture—then curtains and blinds will close automatically.

The Grafik Eye system also means that the home is made more safe and secure. At night, if anyone passes through the gates of the property, lighting is activated to illuminate the pathway, ensuring safe passage to the home. While the car is being parked up and the owners make their way into the home, the system sets the interior lighting to "welcome mode." At the same time, the exterior lighting fades to "occupation mode." All of this happens without any interaction from the residents. When the residents have to leave the house unoccupied, the property is guarded by a security system and programmed lighting that replicates the effect of the property being occupied.

Architecture and design consultancy AJ Browne and Co integrated a Leax automated lighting control system into its design for a private house in London's Holland Park. Director Anthony Browne says: "You can set the most extraordinary of scenes with the system." AJ Browne's interior designer, Thea Haddad, explains that each room is controlled by a scene-setting plate that allows you to achieve various moods throughout the day, simply at the press of a button.→

Supplier   Simon Cope of
audio-visual
consultants Martin
Kleiser (suppliers of
Lutron products)

Year   2001

Location   Private residence,
London, UK

When renovations were undertaken
on this property—located in one of
London's most exclusive areas—the
developer was keen to fuse the
property's 19th-century architecture
with 21st-century technology. Lutron's
HomeWorks Interactive was chosen
as a sophisticated, state-of-the-art
system capable of creating a host of
lighting "scenes" throughout the
property—indoors and out.

Intelligent lighting, whether in the form of a dimmer, individual fitting, entire room, or whole-house control system, all tap into the demand for more atmospheric domestic spaces. There is also a host of other plus points when it comes to incorporating intelligent lighting into the home. The single wall-mounted or remote keypad control, for example, negates the need for a wall full of individual switches and dimmers. One discreet control panel, or indeed no wall panel at all, is surely preferable, reducing wall clutter and allowing focus to fall on more aesthetically pleasing design elements.

Some intelligent lighting can be programmed, giving two distinct benefits. Firstly, programmable lighting, as Lutron's John Niebel says: "Eliminates the tedious task of setting the home lighting correctly for daily activities, bedtime, or special occasions more than once." Secondly, set lighting can provide a home with added security, making it safer by automatically turning on landscape and security lighting each night. Niebel goes on to explains that intelligent lighting can also "memorize a home's actual lighting usage patterns, which can be replayed when the homeowner is away. This unique feature allows for a realistic appearance of activity that standard timers cannot achieve." The system can also be linked to a home's security system: in the event of an alarm, interior lights turn on, illuminating a safe exit, while exterior lights flash, drawing the attention of passersby.

Intelligent lighting is proving that visions of the future are now very much a reality. What was science fiction even a few years ago is now science fact. The technology now exists and is reliable enough to allow almost anything you could want. That is, rooms that are alive, but with lighting that costs less and consumes less energy.

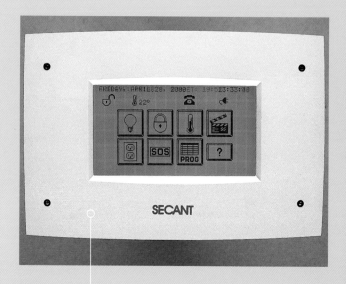

SECANT

Designer   Secant
Distributor   Cardio UK
Year   1995 (USA); 1997
                  (Europe); 2000 (UK)
Dimensions   H 46 cm (17.94in),
                  W 25cm (9.75in),
                  D 9cm (3.51in)
Materials   Plastic
Photography   Cliff Kent

For many home automation systems, a control panel such as this acts as the central hub. The panel can control functions such as heating and security as well as lighting.

Supplier   Simon Cope of
               audio-visual
               consultants Martin
               Kleiser (suppliers of
               Lutron products)
Year   2001
Location   Private residence,
               London, UK

Lutron's HomeWorks Interactive has been installed throughout this London property, including the bathroom, to meet functional as well as atmospheric lighting requirements.

Spotlight on:
Isometrix Lighting + Design

In the late 1990s, eminent designer Philippe Starck and hotel owner Ian Schrager were working on a design for St Martins Lane Hotel in London. Starck had a particular vision in mind when it came to the lighting—especially in the guests' bedrooms. Coming from the standpoint that color and light have a special relationship and that, when fused, they can have a direct bearing on emotion (ideas embodied in color therapy theories; see pages 36-37, 46–47), Starck wanted a system that was capable of emitting color-changing light so that guests could choose their surrounding ambient lighting color to suit their mood. The resulting effect had to have a major influence on the room's appearance, and thus the lighting had to be a dominant feature. But—and here was the real challenge—the lighting equipment also had to be concealed.

With offices in Hong Kong, London, and Paris, Isometrix is a company that has long been conscious that lighting is not solely about function but is also connected with mood and emotion. The company's innovative and versatile approach to lighting, coupled with its awareness that lighting has the capability to change a room and create different moods, made it the ideal candidate to fulfill Starck's brief.

After researching what color-change lighting equipment was available on the market, Isometrix concluded that what Starck wanted didn't yet exist, so it set about creating a bespoke solution. Some two years' research and development later, Colourwash was born.

It might be small in profile, but a Colourwash unit packs a big punch in terms of its lighting capabilities. It offers a pure wash of colored light, with the choice between selecting color manually, or letting the unit automatically cycle through 256 colours in time spans ranging from one to 128 minutes. A single controller is capable of operating an unlimited number of units, and the units themselves can be combined to suit specific wall lengths.

Colourwash units were installed in each of the white, spartan bedrooms of St Martins Lane Hotel, concealed within ceiling coves above the beds and designed to illuminate the walls and throw color across the white Egyptian cotton bedding. Guests can easily select their color of choice via controllers placed beside the luxurious beds.→

Designer	Isometrix Lighting + Design
Year	2000
Dimensions	L 91.8cm (35.8in) or 121.8cm (47.5in)
Materials	Aluminum, stainless steel, dichroic glass, borosilicate glass

Born from a vision that Philippe Starck had for St Martins Lane Hotel, Isometrix's Colourwash has gone on to prove a popular choice in a host of environments. This sleek system, designed to be hidden from view so only the lighting effect is visible, not only offers the possibility of colored light, but the opportunity to change the color emitted as desired.

Highlights

○ In bedrooms, ceiling coves above the bed or storage areas either side of the bed can be ideal "hiding places" for color-changing fittings

○ Incorporate color-changing lighting into rooms with neutral décor.

○ Having the choice to wash a room in different colors means you have a space that can be colored to suit different moods.

Designer Philippe Starck
Architect Harper Mackay
Year 1999
Location The 250 hotel suites in St Martins Lane Hotel, London, UK

Isometrix's original Colourwash Lighting system was installed in the bedrooms of the St Martins Lane Hotel to allow clients to select washes of colored light easily. As every guest can select the color within their rooms, when you view the floor-to-ceiling glass façade of the hotel from street level, the effect is a patchwork of color.

Inspired by a stay at St Martins Lane Hotel, a client of designer Kate Beard wished to create a similar effect in her bedroom at home. With space and ceiling heights at a premium, the equally elegant but more affordable compromise was to use Colourwash to uplight the space, with the unit housed in the void between the custom-built storage areas either side of the bed and headboard. In the St Martins Lane bedrooms, Colourwash is adjusted via a wall-mounted control, but for this brief Beard used Isometrix's Orbiball—a tennis ball-sized, spherical controller allowing remote access.

It is not only residential interiors that have exploited intelligent colored lighting to great effect: Colourwash has been installed in a host of other environments. Its inclusion at the pioneering Beatrice Tate School in London's Bethnal Green, a school that provides education for a wide age range of children with either physical or mental disabilities, is testimony to how colored light can have distinct therapeutic qualities. Isometrix was approached during the initial design stages of the school's redevelopment program, which was to include a hydrotherapy pool and two multisensory studios. The brief was to provide functional yet adjustable creative light within both sensory studios. Sensory Room One has the option of shutting off all exterior light, and one wall of Colourwash lighting effectively illuminates the whole area. The larger studio contains two areas that can be controlled individually, or linked together to change color automatically—either in time or just out of time to create a wave effect, moving from one side of the room to the other.

Designer Kate Beard
Year 2002
Location Private residence

Kate Beard's client wanted her own bedroom to be lit just like the hotel bedrooms at St Martins Lane Hotel. Colourwash was installed in a slightly different way to suit the room's dimensions.

Trade secrets

"Dimmers are the easiest and simplest way of incorporating a degree of lighting control into your home. A simple rotary control will allow you to change the ambience of any room and is a relatively inexpensive way to enhance your décor. Installing a single-circuit dimmer is relatively simple, and within the grasp of any keen DIYer. Whole-room controls require more thought and usually involve the use of an electrician."
John Niebel *Lutron Electronics*

Consider incorporating lighting with its own internal dimmer. Many light fittings are being designed with this facility, meaning that light can be lowered when an ambient light is desired, or turned full-on for functional lighting.

Include table and incidental lamps when adding lighting controls. They are an important part of your lighting and are often overlooked.

"When considering intelligent lighting designed to wash color into a room, bear in mind that the surface to be illuminated must be white, although it is effective to illuminate textured surfaces, such as painted brick."
Chris Miller *Isometrix Lighting + Design*

Distributor	Franklite
Year	2001
Dimensions	Wall light H 18.5cm (7.22in), W 10cm (3.9in); pendant drop 59cm–78cm (23.01in–30.42in), W 70.5cm (27.5in); floor lamp H 1780cm (694.2in)
Materials	Satin nickel and chrome finish, 24% lead crystal glass

We're used to seeing lead crystal in traditional chandeliers, but in the Cubit collection, cubes of lead crystal glass have been applied in single rows within each fitting, tying in with their linear designs. The floor lamp shown has an integral "on", "off", and "dimmer" switch for ultimate control of light levels; the table lamp, too, can be dimmed to create a more intimate environment.

**Lighting
Designer**   Studio Lux
**Interior
Designer**   Dorian Muncey
Year   1989
Location   Capitol Hill
condominium, Seattle,
USA
Photography   Dorian Muncey

In this dining area, Studio Lux
wanted to create a lighting scheme
that would both highlight particular
features in the space, such as the wall
and table art, and create flexible
lighting to suit different moods. The
former was achieved through the
use of integrated spotlights, while
general lighting comes from recessed
downlighters. All of the lights can
be controlled by a lighting control
system, allowing light levels to
be altered to produce different,
sometimes dramatic, effects
for entertaining.

off the wall

 integral

art

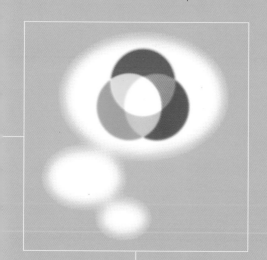

Off the wall:
Integral

When space is at a premium and we want to keep rooms as uncluttered as possible, filling a room with both lighting and furniture can seem inefficient and inelegant. Until relatively recently, we've had no choice but to incorporate furniture and lighting as separate elements, and accept that their inclusion might make a room feel smaller. Both, after all, have a key role to play in an interior décor scheme.

Rather than having a piece of furniture that is then lit separately, from a wall- or ceiling-mounted fixture, or a freestanding lamp, why not fuse the two and place the light source within the furniture? A growing number of furniture designers are proposing this as a space-efficient, design-savvy solution, designing funky furniture forms and then adding lighting as an integral element to create pieces of illuminated furniture.

It would be wrong, however, to assume that illuminated furniture is a new concept—such pieces were being produced back in the 1960s and 70s. Verner Panton's Illumesa table (see page 118), made from plastic and lit from within by a standard bulb, is a classic example from this era. Produced in 1970, the table presented a simple solution—rather than having a table with a separate table lamp, Illumesa is an integral table lamp. Why Panton's creation wasn't followed by a host of similar products was probably down to a number of factors. Not least of these was that plastic, or materials of that ilk, fell out of favor, being regarded as a cheap, less sophisticated, furniture material when compared to finishes such as wood and glass. Today, however, plastic and its various derivatives, such as polycarbonate and polyethylene, are back in favor. These materials offer a translucent finish ideal for transmitting light, and furniture designers are utilizing them to create chairs, tables, and other illuminated furniture pieces.→

Designer   Ben Rousseau
Year   2002
Dimensions   L 200cm (78in),
                 W 80cm (31.2in),
                 H 70cm (27.3in)
Materials   Black American
                 walnut, Perspex,
                 leather, aluminum
Photography Jake Curtis

The Electrowerkz sofa, which complements the designer's Electrowerkz table (see page 75), features a track of LED lights positioned close together so they appear to be a continuous strip. Light beams across the legs of the seated person and from underneath the sofa. The use of rich materials and deep seats create a sense of luxury, whether the lighting is on or off.

Designer	Doug Harper
Year	2002
Dimensions	L 200cm (78in),
	W 50cm (19.5in),
	H 60cm (23.4in)
Materials	Polyethylene base,
	satin stainless steel
Photography	Stephen Brayne

Doug Harper Furniture's Litables range, introduced in 2000 and expanded in 2002, comprises a number of pieces. Each is internally lit, offering the best of both worlds—furniture that is also a light source. Playing with the current trend toward spacious, modular sofas that wrap around the corner of the room, Harper has come up with his own twist—an illuminated modular sofa. For additional comfort, the sofa can have leather seating and backrests.

BoBo Design, based in England, is a firm specializing in illuminated furniture. Perspex, a wonderfully translucent material that allows for an even distribution of light, has been used to create pieces such as Glonuts (see page 132): dual-function forms that can be used as seats or storage. The human eye, as one half of the firm's husband-and-wife design team, Nick Gant, says, "is naturally drawn to light. By integrating it into the fabric that surrounds us, and sculpting light through our domestic possessions, we subconsciously feel its benefits."

This is one of the main reasons why Gant's firm, and a growing number of other companies, are pushing ahead with creating hybrid forms that tap into the trend for space-poor, function-rich pieces.

Abbi Kiki, also based in England, creates integrally lit furniture (see pages 78–79). Her product range includes illuminated coffee tables and wall tiles. Kiki says: "The main advantage of specifying an illuminated piece of furniture is the dual functionality it offers, as the object — whether it is a table, sideboard, counter, etc — also provides a source of light."

When we consider that lighting generally comes into play at night, and so is relatively redundant until darkness falls, incorporating lighting into a piece of furniture means that the piece has a role to play both day and night. The extra beauty that lighting can bring to furniture is a key reason why British lighting and interior designer Ben Rousseau (see pages 48–49) mixes the two: "Some people use lighting as a feature. I want to go a step further by giving an item a new identity. I want that item to look good in its own right, but then I want it to say something else when the light is on."

Where furniture is lit from within, homeowners can use this as the only light source in a room when a more intimate environment is desired. This mood lighting effect can be further enhanced by color, either in the light source or the material of the form. Some items have color-changing lighting to make them even more eye-catching. Pieces do not, however, need to be evenly illuminated throughout — an item in which lighting is incorporated in a more subtle way can offer a more discreet effect. Rousseau's Electrowerkz table and sofa, for instance (see pages 72 and right), feature a subtle line of light to define the pieces.→

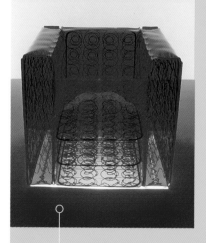

Designer Ennemlaghi
Year 2000
Dimensions H 72cm (28.08in),
W 80cm (31.2in),
D 78cm (30.42in)
Materials PVC, steel springs

Ennemlaghi's Cube Chair uses the concept of integrating inside and outside, with the transparent saddlestitched PVC skin revealing the chair's inner metal springs. The "inside and outside" concept is further enhanced when the chair is placed on a lightbox or has fluorescent lights inserted into the frame itself, causing both the chair and its inner workings to glow.

Designer Ben Rousseau
Year 2001
Dimensions L 90cm (35.1in),
W 90cm, H 30cm
(11.7in)
Materials Black American
walnut, clear Perspex,
reactive blue Perspex,
aluminum
Photography Jake Curtis

Ben Rousseau is a designer whose work focuses on lighting-based furniture and interiors. Such work includes the Electrowerkz table, of which there are two versions. In the first, shown here, fluorescent tubes emit UV light around the table's edge (made up of a mix of clear and blue Perspex). The result is a calming glow that bounces off the floor and surroundings. When the lighting is turned off, you still have an elegant-looking table. The second version of the table uses an LED color-changing system from Colour Kinetics, opening up a variety of possibilities — for instance, the table can be washed in a different color every five seconds.

Chairs and tables might be the most obvious candidates for integral lighting, but it can be used in more imaginative places, too. An illuminated bathroom suite is stunning, and even flooring can be lit this way. Neither is illuminated furniture necessarily limited to interior use. Some lit furniture (though certainly not all, so always check manufacturers' guidelines) can be used in the garden as well. Doug Harper's Litables range of illuminated cubes, cylinders, chairs, and sofas (see page 73), with special spiky rubber seats and backs for comfort, are perfect for alfresco entertaining.

Illuminated furniture might have received a cool reception in the 1960s, but in the 21st century it's a hot design concept; an exciting strand of furniture design that responds perfectly to the needs of small urban spaces, but that can also be dramatic in more spacious surrounds.

Designer Piero De Marchis, De Marchis Sergison
Interior Builder Silver Interiors
Location Private residence, London, UK
Year 2002
Photography Richard Seymour

London-based Piero De Marchis wanted to make a focal point of this drawing room's Lalique glass table. What better way to achieve this than by integrally lighting the table? Buried uplights from Genesis were carefully spaced so as to illuminate the limbs of the table—without dazzling diners too much. The result is an amazing glow.

Designer WaveDecor
Year 2002
Dimensions H 43cm (16.77in), L 110cm (42.9in), D 60cm (23.4in)
Materials Chromium steel tube, acrylic

WaveDecor's WaveTable (shown here) and WaveLiteTable bring new meaning to the table lamp. Composed of acrylic vanes that have in-built fluorescence, the tables are lit in two ways. While the WaveLiteTable is internally lit, WaveTable comes to life when a single spotlight is shone onto its surface.

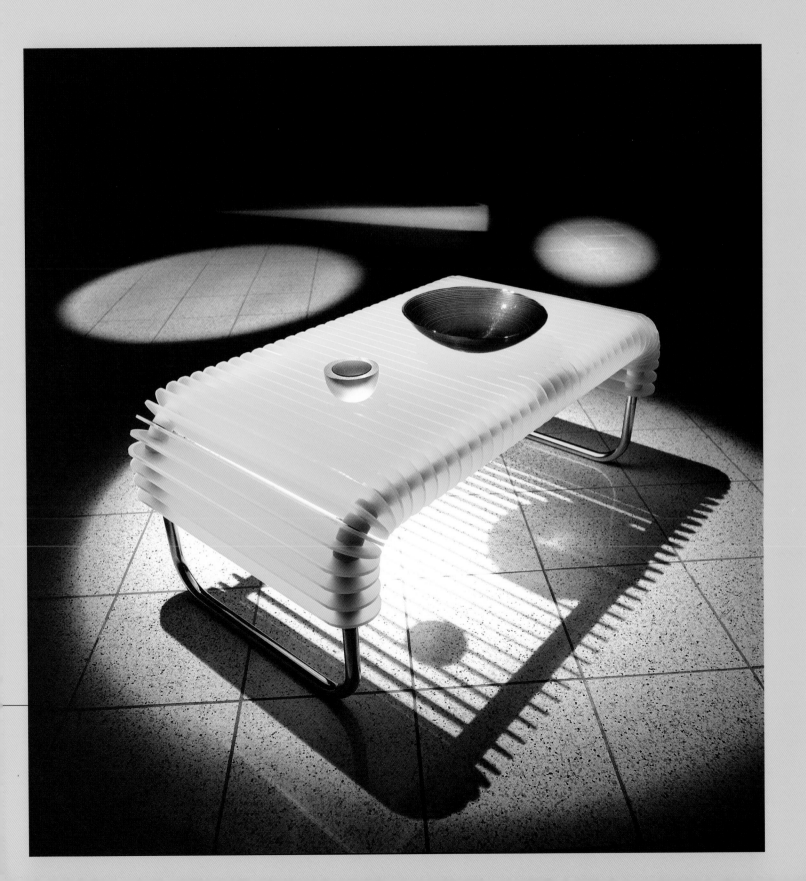

Spotlight on:
Abbi Kiki, kiki UK

When we choose furniture for our homes, we do so bearing in mind how it will complement existing pieces in a room. Will the color work within the space? Will the design complement other elements in the scheme? The same checklist must be adhered to when contemplating incorporating illuminated furniture into a commercial interior. As kiki UK's work at Ali Cats Bar and Light Bar show, it is perfectly possible for integrally lit pieces to have a direct relationship with an interior in its entirety. In both cases, pieces by kiki UK tie in with particular themes in the décor of the bars, and so are cohesive with the overall design ethos.

In the Ali Cats Bar, Abbi Kiki redesigned lighting for the entire bar area. It had been previously a dingy basement space, "Brimming with the characteristics of mysterious, dark alleyways." With a limited budget, Kiki's solution was to tailor pieces from her standard product portfolio to make them unique to this interior. She took her illuminated Classic Lucci wall tiles and used them as lightboxes, inset with photographs of local alleyways. She adapted her integrally lit Lucci Co coffee tables with a special graffiti finish. Finally, she took the trashcans that were already part of the décor and added illuminated lids to them to turn them into tabletops. The trashcan lids were decorated with photos of cats with text added to create narrative.

The Light Bar project offered Kiki a chance to provide lighting solutions for a brand new establishment, the directors of which were keen to create something individual, using lighting in such a major way that it influenced the name of the bar itself. Kiki's brief was to create "something cool, relaxed, different, colorful, warm, and cheerful." Rather than create a completely bespoke solution, which would have incurred greater costs, she set about working on subtle applications that could easily be incorporated in the standard products available. As with the Ali Cats Bar, when it came to integrally lit pieces, slight changes were made to Kiki's illuminated coffee tables and wall tiles. Throughout the bar and restaurant, red was the starting point for Kiki's theme.

Designer	Abbi Kiki, kiki UK
Year	1999
Location	Ali Cats Bar, Brighton, UK

Kiki redesigned the lighting for the entire bar area, tailoring a number of her lighting pieces to make them unique to the interior. Her Classic Lucci wall tiles were used as lightboxes with special images inserted into the tiles, and her Lucci Co coffee tables had a special graffiti finish applied. Other lit elements were introduced to tie in with the bar's name, such as a row of trashcans with illuminated lids.

Highlights

○ Match the color of furnishing with lights.

○ Focus light on the key task of the space, such as eating.

○ Using colored gels on lights can convey instant mood.

Designer Abbi Kiki, kiki UK
Year 1998
Location Light Bar, Cambridge, UK

As the owner wanted the color red to predominate, Kiki included two of her designs—Lucci Co illuminated coffee tables and Classic Lucci illuminated wall tiles—in this color. Leather sofas softened the area, ensuring that it didn't become too saturated in light, while Kiki introduced other interior elements, such as special troughs for the storage of glasses, to continue the color theme.

Spotlight on:
Suck UK

Colored lighting, has long been the mainstay of the nightclub world, but this lighting can be applied in the home, without necessarily inciting us to dance.

Suck UK's illuminated coffee table is a club-inspired piece, used in bars, restaurants, clubs, and private homes to create a perfect social ambience. Designed to be versatile, the table is packed with innovative features. While similar furniture designs light the table's surface, independent controllers located on this table's leg offer the choice between illuminating the toughened glass top, its underside, or both elements. Users can choose from more than 200 colors, through the use of fluorescent light tubes with interchangeable filters. The table is available in various measurements, and graphics can be chosen for the tabletop to further customize the piece.

Interior designers employed to style metropolitan show homes are wise to the benefits of integral lighting design, as innovative design inspires aspirational desires. The show home of Tanners Yard, London, was fitted out with these principles in mind, and they installed Suck UK's coffee table in the living area. The table is a functional item, with a magical edge.

Highlights

○ Use illuminated furniture to replicate the social atmosphere of a club-like environment.

○ Color-changing illuminated furniture allows you to select a color conducive to a particular mood.

○ An integrally lit piece of furniture makes a very modern statement—lit or unlit.

Designer Suck Uk
Interior Peggy Prendeville,
Designers Bella Whiteley
Architects Yeates Design
Year 2001
Location Tanners Yard show
home, London, UK

The designers of this show home chose Suck UK's illuminated coffee table to grab the attention of potential homebuyers, as it oozes contemporary style. The user can opt for three different lighting modes (as shown opposite) and also play with different colors.

Trade secrets

→ Don't forget how other light fittings can be used in conjunction with integrally lit furniture to create an intimate atmosphere.

→ Choose colors both for their aesthetic value, and for their therapeutic benefits (see pages 36-37, 46–47). Consider how an illuminated piece of furniture could work on this level.

→ "Consider special maintenance issues when it comes to illuminated furniture—can it take only a certain amount of weight, for instance?"
Doug Harper *Doug Harper Furniture*

→ Most illuminated furniture currently on offer needs plugging in. This has obvious implications for how and where such pieces are used. Some designers offer a middle ground. Doug Harper's Litables pieces, for example, do not necessarily need to be plugged in, but can be permanently wired to prepared positions for remote switching.

The living room is an obvious area in which to incorporate illuminated furniture, but other rooms can also benefit from the inclusion of integrated lighting.

→ Bespoke solutions are generally more expensive, but can be a great way of ensuring that your home has a unique piece that perfectly complements your décor and space.

Designer	Rare Basics
Year	2002
Dimensions	H up to 130cm (50.7in), W 40cm (15.6in)
Materials	Polyethylene

These Colour Changing Illuminated Columns and Cubes were initially designed for the retail industry, but are equally applicable in the home. Each column or cube is independently controlled by a single light source that can be set at one color, or morph through a sequence of color changes. As with many other illuminated forms, these pieces can be used as standalone lights or serve as innovative display systems. When the surface of the columns or cubes is used as a shelf or table, items placed on top absorb the illumination and color emitted.

Designer Sottini
Year 2001
Dimensions Close-coupled WC
suite H 81cm (31.59in),
L 67cm (26.13in),
W 37.5cm (14.63in);
back-to-wall
WC suite: (concealed
cistern) H 39cm
(15.21in), W 51cm
(19.89in), D 38.5cm
(15.02in); washbasin
H 85cm (33.2in),
W 46cm (17.94in),
D 55cm (21.45in); bath
H 60cm (23.4in),
W 169.5cm (66.11in),
D 79.5cm (31.01in)
Materials Acrylic, porcelain

The Philosophy Nightlight suite of
bathrooms emits a soft, candle-like
glow. The porcelain suite, comprising
bath, basin, and toilet, is enclosed in
a transparent acrylic sheet, lit by soft
LEDs. The result is a luxurious, subtle
illumination to enhance mood.

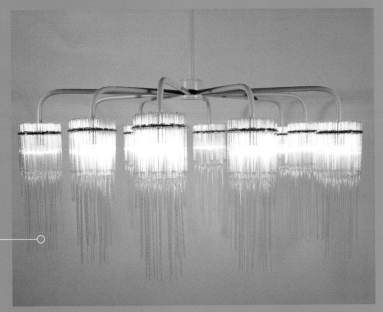

Off the wall:
Art

Some elements in a room are there because they meet specific functional demands; others are less practical but are included because of their aesthetic qualities. Art, whether in the form of a painting, a print, or a sculpture, obviously falls into the latter category. When the sun sets, how do we ensure that these prized possessions can be appreciated? Traditionally, the solution has been to use accent lighting—picture lights, strategically placed above a wall-hung work of art, for instance, or spotlights angled to highlight a sculpture. While there's no doubt that this is a very effective way of illuminating art, used in museums around the world, art can have a much closer relationship to light. Many innovators in the field are experimenting with a hybrid form of light and art, which can simply be described as "lit art."

One form of lit art has, of course, been with us for some time—the chandelier. Highly decorative and generally made from crystal, the chandelier has long been a striking visual statement and status symbol. But chandeliers are often associated with grand, stately homes and can look less appropriate in more modest interiors. Aware that such an attitude prevailed, many lighting designers have created modern twists on the traditional archetype. Through the use of different materials—or the use of traditional crystal in a less conventional manner—and various light sources, including the increasingly popular LEDs and fiber optics, chandeliers in different shapes and sizes are available to suit even the most modern home.→

Designer   Tom Kirk
Year   2002
Dimensions   H 100cm (39in), W 90cm (35.1in), D 90cm. Glass filaments L 1.7cm (0.66in)/2.3cm (0.9in)/2.7cm (1.05in)
Materials   Steel and glass

Tom Kirk's GS Chandelier is a modern take on the traditional chandelier—always famed for its visual presence in any setting and its ability to work as a piece of art in a room. GS comes in a number of multiarm combinations. Slender glass straws hang from these arms.

Designer   The Bradley Collection
Year   1998
Dimensions   H 26cm (10.14in), W 72cm (28.08in)
Materials   Polished steel (also available in waxed steel)

The Beehive chandelier—complemented by a matching double wall sconce and curtain finial—shows how metal can be used to create all manner of contemporary fittings, combining a disciplined style with a lean profile.

Designer	Tord Boontje
Year	2001
Dimensions	Garland length 145cm (56.55in), finished light approx H 40cm (15.6in), W 20cm (7.8in), D 20cm
Materials	Stainless steel

The Wednesday Light fuses lighting and art. Supplied without the wire, lampholder, or bulb, the light comes as a garland that is attached to the wire above with a simple clip and then wrapped around the bulb—a bit like flower arranging. As long as the fittings used are applicable for exterior use, Wednesday can be used in an outdoor setting.

Many lighting designers assert that, as light and art share similarities, it makes sense to fuse the two. A light does not have the same design constraints as other interior objects; there is no need for it to be ergonomic as it's rarely handled at all, a bit like art. Many designers offer lit sculptural pieces, many of which are ideally suited for positioning on a tabletop, shelf, or mantelpiece—areas where traditional sculptures would generally be placed. Lit art is often as appropriate for the garden as inside the home. Wherever they are destined for use, all these lit pieces are designed with dual functionality in mind, emitting a warm, ambient light in the evening while retaining their aesthetic appeal during the day.

While smaller integrally lit pieces, as well as pendants and chandeliers, can be seen as alternatives to traditional sculptures, there are lit art options that can be used in place of wall-mounted paintings or prints. One of the main limitations of standard paintings and prints is that, while the images displayed obviously appeal to the owner, such images are frozen in time. Some wall-mounted work crosses the boundaries between art, design, and light, incorporating the idea of evolution, with sequenced color changes and textured surfaces.

Lit wall art can also have a more powerful presence in a room than traditional options when, rather than being a flat piece of wall art, it projects from the wall in some way. 3D effects have been used in a number of designs, making the pieces far more eye-catching, and standing out both day and night. These 3D effects also offer more interactivity because of their tactile quality—people are drawn to touch them, discover what materials the works are made of, and how the lighting has been incorporated.

Designer	Jeremy Lord, The Colour Light Co
Year	2002
Dimensions	H 40cm (15.6in), W 40cm, D 4.5cm (1.76in)
Materials	Perspex front panel, aluminum frame

The Colour Light Co's Chromascreen L400 color-changing panels of light can be arranged in small groups or spread out to occupy larger areas. Up to eight panels can be operated together. The panels are designed to generate a never-ending sequence of color, at the speed of the owner's choice. This infinite range of colors is possible because of the incorporation of LED technology.

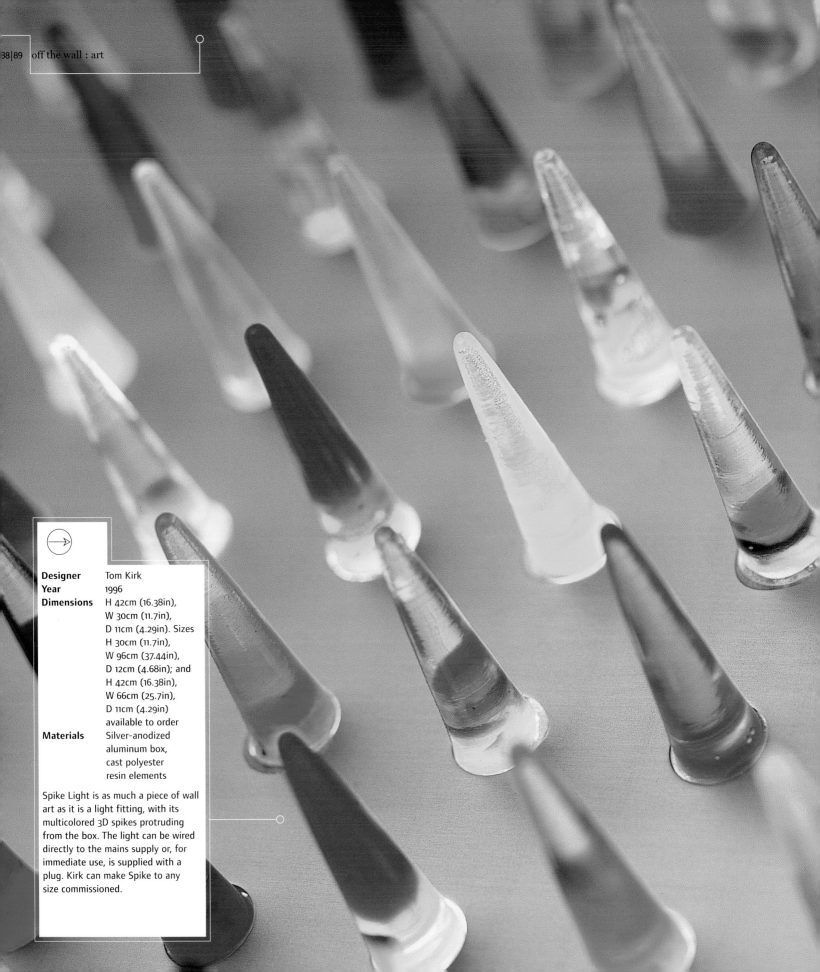

Designer	Tom Kirk
Year	1996
Dimensions	H 42cm (16.38in), W 30cm (11.7in), D 11cm (4.29in). Sizes H 30cm (11.7in), W 96cm (37.44in), D 12cm (4.68in); and H 42cm (16.38in), W 66cm (25.7in), D 11cm (4.29in) available to order
Materials	Silver-anodized aluminum box, cast polyester resin elements

Spike Light is as much a piece of wall art as it is a light fitting, with its multicolored 3D spikes protruding from the box. The light can be wired directly to the mains supply or, for immediate use, is supplied with a plug. Kirk can make Spike to any size commissioned.

Spotlight on:
Sharon Marston, UK

Sharon Marston has established herself as one of the leading figures of the British lighting design scene. Her work, a wonderful fusion of light and sculpture, has been used to create a focal point in a host of environments, from retail areas to private homes. Marston's background in fashion, theater, and contemporary dance has had a direct influence on the pieces she produces, all of which have been designed to be "visually innovative."

One way of achieving this is through the use of unusual materials. Marston's lit art collection of freestanding table and floor lamps, pendants, and chandeliers is made from an array of materials, including polypropylene, mono filament, woven nylon, glass, steel, cotton, and Perspex. By mixing such materials, the results are objects that also have a degree of tactility.

Lighting might be key to Marston's pieces, but she is keen that this is a hidden element, which doesn't detract or take attention away from each piece's unique look. In many instances, fiber optics have proved ideal, as using them means that there are many points of light coming from the one light source, dispersing light throughout the piece. Marston explains: "Integrated into the design form, they become part of the structure, become one."

Consider the fiber-optic chandeliers that Marston supplied for a private house in London, designed by architectural and design consultancy AJ Browne and Co. One was installed in the entrance area; the second was for the guestroom. The latter space featured a very minimal, clean design. In such a context, the chandelier "stands out because of its unusual abstract and intense shape, and brings warmth into the room."

The homeowner was eager to make lighting a main feature of the home, and was especially interested in light sculptures. AJ Browne therefore incorporated fittings available off the shelf—such as Marston's chandeliers—with bespoke design solutions, to make the interior of the house a "living light art—an art lightbox."

Designer	Sharon Marston
Year	2002
Location	Private residence, London, UK
Photography	Gillian Cargill

Marston was commissioned by architectural consultancy AJ Browne to supply her fiber-optic lit chandelier for a private house.

Designer	Sharon Marston
Year	2000
Dimensions	On specification
Materials	Steel unit, acrylic, Perspex
Photography	Gillian Cargill

The Optic Wall Light protrudes from its steel casing to create a wonderful piece of 3D illuminated wall art. Rather than limiting choice to a standard wall light, Marston offers clients the opportunity to have a bespoke version in the size and shape of their choice.

Highlights

○ Use lit art as the a focal point in a room instead of a traditional sculpture or artwork.

○ A piece of lit art can bring warmth and color into a space.

○ Fiber optics are an ideal light source to use within lit art as they are a hidden and become one with the decorative piece.

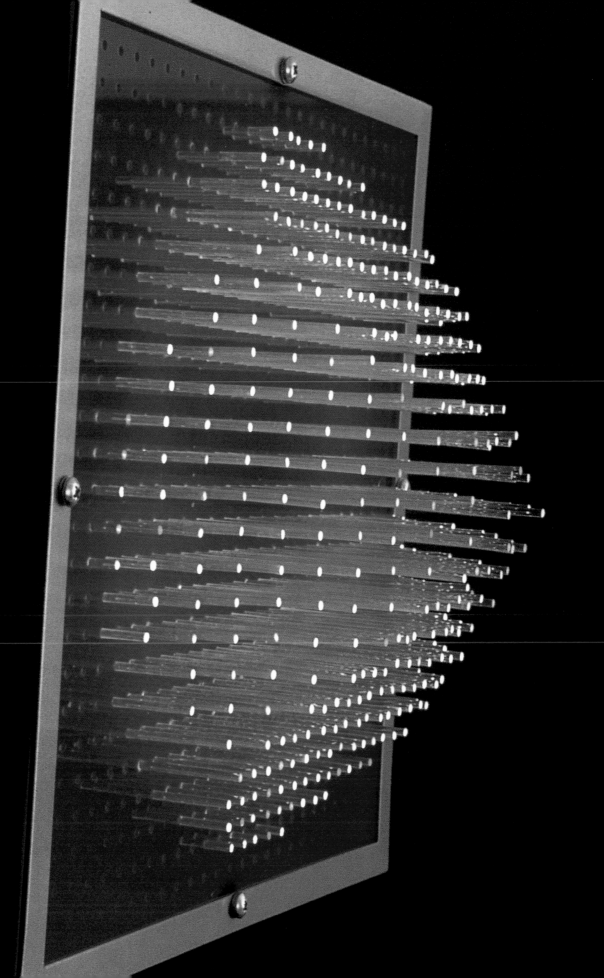

Spotlight on:
Georgia Scott Designs

Nature often serves as the inspiration when it comes to freestanding, integrally lit sculptures—especially those destined for decorative use. Many pieces by London-based lighting designer Georgia Scott draw on natural forms such as plants, seed pods, icicles, and the skeletons of trees. More often than not, these pieces are handmade, as opposed to mass-manufactured, to keep them more sculptural.

In many instances, the objects are woven into their nature-inspired shapes using materials such as aluminum and copper mesh. Such materials offer malleability—essential for creating intricate forms—and also present Scott with an opportunity, in her words, to "play with light, and achieve different qualities of light through the materials."

The results of Scott's experimentation with lighting are pieces such as Flower Shower, where hand-folded mesh flower shapes are subtly lit by fiber optics. The piece incorporates a sparkle filter, so the glass fiber optics move and create a shimmering effect. In Flame Light, a piece inspired by fall leaves, copper mesh has been hand-folded into flame-shaped leaves. The heat-treated patina of the copper gently diffuses light to bring out the red tones of the leaves.

It is clear that organically inspired forms don't only meet the needs of lighting and art. Plants and flowers are short-lived and demand upkeep and hospitable conditions: a lit sculpture can act as an illuminated floral or plant replacement, especially in areas such as basements, where there is little natural light.

Highlights

 Why not sculpt your own wire-mesh or copper-wire shades? Natural or industrially minimal forms can be created quite simply.

○ Integrally lit sculptures are ideal for gloomy rooms lacking in natural light.

Designer	Georgia Scott Designs
Year	2002
Dimensions	To specification
Materials	Hand-folded aluminum mesh

Georgia Scott's Flower Shower pendant presents a shower of fiber optics twinkling through hand-folded mesh flower shapes. Suitable for a variety of areas, especially stairwells, the piece can be made in different sizes to order.

Designer	Georgia Scott Designs
Year	2000
Dimensions	To specification
Materials	Copper mesh

The Flame Light is made from hand-folded copper mesh, heated to make it more malleable, to produce this wonderfully sculptural piece. With the red of the copper mesh "flames" and the light within like a burning ember, the piece almost seems alive.

Designer Georgia Scott Designs
Year 1998
Dimensions Floor version H 90cm
(35.1in), W 30cm
(11.7in); table version
H 40cm (15.6in),
W 30cm (11.7in)
Materials Aluminum mesh

Georgia Scott has taken aluminum
mesh and hand-folded it into 3D
shapes to create these wonderful
Spike Lights, which are reminiscent of
exotic plants. While the lights
themselves are unarguably eye-
catching, they also create wonderful
lighting effects, casting ethereal
patterns onto walls and ceilings.

Trade secrets

Modern chandelier forms on the market can be used in homes of all sizes and rooms of varying interior styles.

"A piece can integrate, complement, as well as transform the ambience of the existing environment. A light installation/sculpture will have strong characteristics, acting as a focus, attracting the eye, and creating a certain ambience depending on the type of lighting, color range, and materials chosen."
Karin Sanner *Global Glass Art*

 Lit art may be more expensive than traditional lighting, but remember that you are paying for a dual-function piece. Add up how much it would cost to buy a piece of art and then a separate light fitting to illuminate this.

 Remember that some lit art can be used in the outdoor room—the garden or yard—as well. It is, of course, imperative that you check the fitting is suitable for use in an exterior setting.

 Consider the overall design of the environment in which a piece is to be placed to ensure that it doesn't "fight" with other elements.

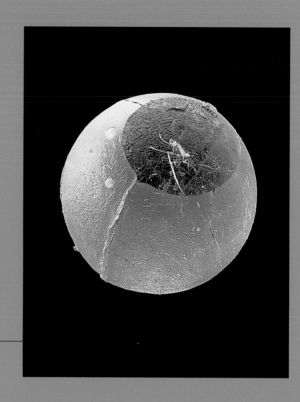

Designer	Karin Sanner and Maria Zulueta, Global Glass Art
Year	2000
Dimensions	D 15cm (5.85in)
Materials	Lead crystal glass

View any of Global Glass Art's pieces during the day and you'd be forgiven for thinking that they have only a decorative role to play in the home as individual works of glass art. The pieces have an attractive presence in a room during the day—the way natural daylight catches on the different forms is quite striking—but they also attract the eye at night, as they are integrally lit. The light is predominantly provided by LEDs.

Designer	Jurgen Bay (distributed by Moooi)
Year	1999
Dimensions	Chandelier and shade H 82cm (31.98in), D 47cm (18.33in); Five-armed chandelier and shade H 75cm (29.25in), D 70cm (27.3in)
Materials	Semitransparent mirror film

Lightshade Shade, part of the Moooi Weer collection, is a unique way of transforming a chandelier and bringing it into the 21st century. The piece comprises a shade made from mirrored film that works to reveal the inner chandelier when the chandelier is lit, and conceal it when it isn't lit. Moooi also supplies the shade on its own, allowing users to give other, older lamps a makeover.

exterior

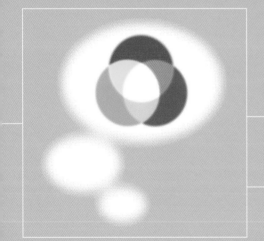

Exterior

The garden or yard has traditionally been a space we have utilized only during the day. We regard it as a haven, a place to spend some quiet time away from the hustle and bustle of our everyday lives. But when the sun sets and the plants and flowers in the yard are cast into darkness, we invariably retreat inside. If you consider the garden as a more integral part of the home, an outdoor room that you can use to entertain, dine, and relax in, then lighting is the key to transforming the space into a nighttime oasis. Instead, try to create a seamless transition between outdoor areas and interiors. Bringing the outside into the house and vice versa gives an overall impression of greater, more flexible space. Achieving this is entirely possible if you apply the lighting schemes from your interior rooms to your outdoor spaces.

Ambient lighting, for instance, can be used within the home in order to achieve a warm, inviting, and relaxing glow. A similar effect can be created outside. Installing a decorative wall fitting onto the side of a home can wash a gentle glow of light onto the building itself and the garden. Such lighting can also be placed on an exterior wall or fence.→

Designer	Bruce Munro
Year	1999
Location	Private garden, Wiltshire, UK

Lighting in the garden isn't just about placing fittings along walkways, on the side of homes, or discreetly within planting, as this lighting installation proves. Lighting designer Bruce Munro wanted to turn this cherry tree in a private walled garden into a distinct feature. Uplighting was used to dramatic effect, while the surrounding space was left unlit to emphasize the tree's natural beauty.

Fittings can be placed in discreet positions within the exterior space. Flora and fauna can provide a great hiding place, creating an ambient glow at night, while also picking out the landscape with a subtle degree of accent lighting. An effective solution is to light the plants and bushes from within, so that the fittings are invisible.

Such an effect is possible because of developments in light sources such as LEDs and fiber optics. Small in size and therefore capable of being housed in small fittings, they are ideal for applications where the fitting remains out of sight while the light emitted packs a powerful punch. Using such sources is also energy-efficient.

Another stunning exterior use of LEDs and fiber optics is to light water features, whether they are positioned around the feature or actually submersed in the water—something that fiber optics make possible. Feng Shui experts assert that including a water element in your home helps to create balance and harmony, so lighting your water feature would surely maximize this.→

Designer   Bruce Munro
Year   2001
Location   Private residence, Caribbean

British lighting designer Bruce Munro positioned linear submersible luminaires on either side of this courtyard pond in the Caribbean to create subtle illumination of the flora and fauna within the pond. The placement of pin-spot downlighting above planters and sculptures is both functional and decorative.

Designer	Mathmos
Year	1999
Dimensions	L 13cm (5.07in), W 9cm (3.51in)
Materials	Polished die-cast zinc, soft-touch thermoplastic, silicone

Part of the Mathmos Mobiles range—so named because every product in the collection uses LEDs and is entirely portable—Aduki is a handheld mobile light that can be either laid flat or hung up, indoors and out. It also changes color—you can either let Aduki move through the color spectrum or freeze the piece on a desired color at the touch of a button.

In drawings and paintings, chiaroscuro (the treatment of light and shade) is a crucial element. The same can be said when approaching lighting in the yard. By bringing light to a specific object and leaving the surrounding space in shade or darkness, that object is given more prominence, becoming a focal point. When it comes to shining light on a particular object or decorative feature in the garden—your favorite plant or tree, for example—there are a number of fittings that can be used. Outdoor versions of up and downlighters are available, for instance. Spotlights are particularly good at providing directional light, as well as providing extra security.

Of course, light doesn't have to be directed onto an object. Just as lit art and illuminated furniture are making their presence known inside the home, it is equally possible to incorporate some of these pieces into the exterior space (although not all—always check the manufacturer's specifications as to whether something is suitable for outdoor use). A lit piece of art creates a stunning focal point, whether it's a traditional sculpture made from a material such as stone, using mainstream lighting (including candles), or one that offers a contemporary twist, fusing unusual materials with forward-thinking light sources.

As exterior lit art comes in a range of shapes and sizes, there are endless possibilities in terms of where it can be positioned, but smaller pieces can be ideal centerpieces for alfresco dining tables—a windproof and less waxy alternative to candles. Inclusion of a dining area in the garden exemplifies the role of the yard as an outdoor room. While lighting can be used to illuminate such an area—whether by way of lit art or more traditional light fittings—there is another way of bringing light to the space. Many designers of integrally lit furniture are able to adapt the materials, cabling, connections, plugs, and so on, to take permanent exterior placement into account.→

Designer	Julie Nelson
Year	2002
Dimensions	Loop II (left) H 60cm (23.4in), W 33M (12.87in), D 28cm (10.92in). Eclipse H 38cm (14.82in), W 35cm (13.65in), D 19cm (6.65in)
Materials	Ceramic stoneware

This collection of outdoor sculptural pieces comprises six ceramic forms, each with its own distinctive characteristic. Handmade in stoneware, the frost-resistant sculptures are accentuated when placed over outdoor floor-mounted lights or candles. The cutout areas of the pieces, especially, come alive when lit.

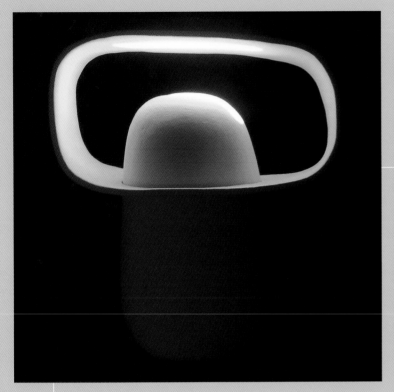

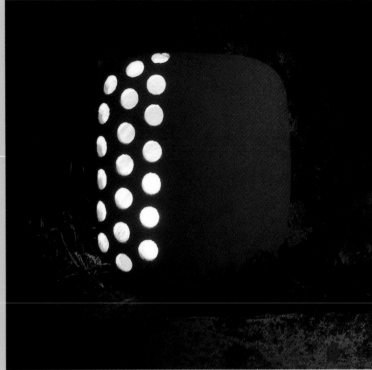

Designer Julie Nelson
Year 2002
Dimensions Loop 1 (top left)
H 42cm (16.38in),
W 39cm (15.21in),
D 18cm (7.02in).
Sponge (top right)
H 33cm (12.87in),
W 28cm (10.92in),
D 18cm (7.02in).
Oblong (right)
H 50cm (19.5in),
W 22cm (8.55in),
D 20cm (7.8in)
Materials Ceramic stoneware

Loop 1 creates a halo-like glow. The
holes in Sponge let the light seep
out. The discrete slits of Oblong
create an elegant path of light.

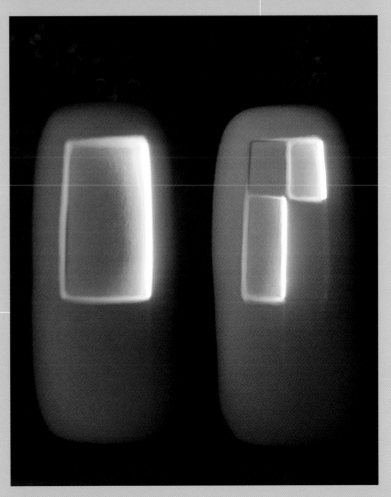

One reason, perhaps, why people have been reticent to install lighting in the garden is because they think there will be lots of tricky wiring involved. While it's true that much exterior lighting does rely on mains connection, installation is often easier than assumed. With solar-powered units, there is also the option of wirefree lighting, which means that the fittings can be repositioned with minimum effort. Inclusion of such fittings has another obvious benefit—solar-powered lights conserve energy from the sun's rays (even on what appears to be a dull day), converting this energy into light. No electricity is used, which is positive news both for household bills and for the environment.

Exterior space isn't always at the rear of a property. We might tend to pass quite quickly through the front exterior space, but lighting can be used here to highlight planting, wash the front of the home itself in a warm glow, and provide navigation through the use of pathway, driveway, and entrance lighting. If the lighting installed in the front, in the rear exterior space, and inside the home is all linked to one control system, then the seamless transition between indoors and out can be achieved easily.

When you appreciate how ambient, accent, energy-efficient lighting, integrally lit art, and furniture can all be utilized in a home's exterior, there's no excuse for not making the most of your outdoor space.

Designer	Bruce Munro
Year	2003
Dimensions	L 50cm (19.5in)
	W 15cm (5.85in)
Materials	Copper

This Moroccan-styled wall sconce was customized from a piece already available in his company's portfolio. The result is a one-off, bespoke light fitting which fuses traditional and contemporary design, and provides a calming glow to the exterior of this conservatory.

Designer Ross Lovegrove for
Luceplan
Year 1998
Dimensions H 28.5cm (11.2in),
W 10.5cm (40.1in);
wall bracket
L 14cm (5.46in)
Materials Polycarbonate

The Pod Lens exterior lighting
system, comprising two different
fittings, can be hung, wall- or
floor-mounted. Available in four
UV-resistant colors, the fittings can
cope with humidity, water, and snow,
and so can add a glow to the garden
throughout the year.

Designer Ross Lovegrove for
Luceplan
Year 1998
Dimensions H 37cm (14.43in),
W 15cm (5.85in)
Materials Aluminum stem,
transparent
polycarbonate head

Many people might be deterred
from using lighting in their yard
because they think it will involve
a lot of complicated wiring. Ross
Lovegrove's Solar Bud lights provide
the perfect solution: lit by solar
energy that powers rechargeable
batteries—no wiring needed.

Spotlight on:
Bruce Munro

Lighting designer Bruce Munro creates innovative lighting solutions for a host of environments. Much of his work is in the residential sector, and fuses lighting and art to powerful effect. Munro also produces stand-alone fittings and integral lighting that is used to create an ambient level of light, or accent a particular area or object of interest. Wherever his residential clients are located—he has worked internationally—Munro is keen to emphasize that residential lighting is about more than the rooms contained within a home's four walls: "I do not think of the exterior as a separate space."

Munro first realized the potential to develop outside lighting solutions when he was approached to light an exterior space for a client. "After inviting several well-known lighting companies to help me light a garden, it became apparent that they were interested only in selling fittings and did not seem to care or understand what they were lighting." Munro used his expertise to come up with his own innovative lighting tricks and fittings.

Integrally lit decorative elements are a speciality of Munro's, especially within alfresco dining areas, where such forms don't only look good but also provide a degree of light conducive to an intimate dining experience. For a decked area in a Caribbean property, for instance, Munro created a number of copper uplighters, mounted onto hand-forged brackets around the deck's perimeter. Light is projected through an aperture in the base plates of these, illuminating the lead crystal shades and creating a warm glow of ambient light. Lead crystal was also used in a table centerpiece that Munro created for a terraced dining area in the South of France. Blue LEDs diffuse light through crystal "icebergs" to create a cooling effect on a hot summer evening.

Water features can be brought alive at night through the use of discreet lighting, as Munro has demonstrated in his work on a courtyard water feature and a waterfall in two properties in the Caribbean. In the former (see page 101), submersible luminaires were placed either side of the pond, capturing glimpses of aquatic life below the lily pads, with pin-spot downlighters above planters and sculptures providing a glow around the pond. When it came to lighting the waterfall, submersible luminaires were positioned at the waterfall's base, to highlight natural breaks and fissures in the rocks, and project lighting effects onto adjacent flora.

Highlights

○ Light your garden's focal point—birdbath, tree, favorite plant—so that it retains its magic at night.

○ Discreet lighting in water features can be used to dramatic effect.

○ Extend your interior living space outside by lighting pathways and seating areas.

Designer	Bruce Munro
Year	2000
Dimensions	H 160cm (62.4in), W 45cm (17.55in, base plate)
Materials	Copper uplighters mounted onto hand-forged brackets, lead crystal shades

This Sea Anemone Luminaire was created to provide exterior ambient lighting for a floating teak deck. Light is projected through an aperture in the base plates, illuminating the individually blown lead crystal diffusing shades.

Designer Bruce Munro
Year 2001
Location Private residence,
Caribbean

This beautiful water feature has
been made even more striking
with the addition of submersible
directional luminaires.

Spotlight on:
David Wilds Patton Lighting Design

When we think about exterior lighting, too often our minds are focused on how the outside space to a rear of a property is lit in order to create an outdoor room that can be made the most of day and night. But exterior spaces to the front of a home also deserve attention when it comes to lighting. We might not use such areas as rooms—after all, they are spaces that we tend to pass through relatively quickly—but lighting here, whether used to ensure a safe passage into the home or in a discreet manner within planting, can be a wonderful addition.

When California-based David Wilds, of David Wilds Patton Lighting Design, was charged with lighting a private residence in Atherton, California (above right), he was acutely aware of how important it was to provide sensitive lighting to the exterior space at the front of the house. On the driveway, Wilds installed special recessed fittings appropriately called Drivestar luminaires (supplied by California-based BK Lighting, a specialist in outdoor architectural lighting). Mounted down the center of the driveway, these fittings help to aid navigation. The small trees that edge the home are also illuminated at night with accent lighting.

In this project, it wasn't only the space around the house, but external parts of the home itself that have been lit. Recessed downlighters have been added on the columns, top steps, and front doors to provide a degree of accent lighting, while luminaires in side stair walls illuminate steps for safety and accent. The front door is lit with a welcoming glow, thanks to the inclusion of two decorative wall sconces.

A careful consideration of exterior lighting can allow a home's architecture and outdoor elements to shine day and night. This point is proved in another residential lighting project handled by David Wilds Patton Lighting Design, this time in California's Woodside district (right). When the sun goes down, surface-mounted wall sconce luminaires provide a mix of downward and upward light distribution to "paint the vertical surfaces," show off the architectural structure, and provide illumination for the two sets of stairs that lead from the upper deck to the lower level. Recessed downlighters wash light onto the lower deck surfaces for parties and general entertainment. The lights inside of the home also contribute to the exterior lighting, glowing from within to create a giant lantern effect.

Highlights
○ Lighting pathways leading to your front door both accent and act as a security feature.

○ Use special features in your front-approach design to place accent lighting.

○ Lighting from inside shines outside, too, so incorporate this into your external lighting design.

Designer	David Wilds Patton Lighting Design
Year	2001
Location	Private residence, Atherton, USA

A number of light fixtures were utilized here, including accent uplighters to show off the various small trees that flank and trim the home, and special recessed fittings mounted down the center of the driveway to aid navigation and add a little sparkle to the drive itself.

Designer David Wilds Patton Lighting Design
Year 2000
Location Private residence, Woodside, USA

A careful consideration for exterior lighting can allow a home's architecture and outdoor elements to shine day and night. In this residential project, when the sun goes down, surface-mounted wall sconce luminaires provide a mix of downward and upward light distribution to show off particular architectural features, and to cast light on the stairs that lead from the upper deck to the lower level.

Trade secrets

Camouflage your exterior fittings so that it is the lit feature rather than the fitting that stands out. LEDs, for instance, can be put in inaccessible areas, and fiber optics are small enough to be hidden from sight.

→ "Accentuate features in the natural landscape— uplighting trees, for instance. You can also layer exterior lighting so as to add or bring out depth."
Phil Riley *The Light Lab*

"Think about creating darkness to emphasize the areas that you want to stand out through light."
Bruce Munro *Lighting designer*

→ "Well lights provide uplighting from a concealed source. Spotlights provide visual interest, and accent on specific plants and architectural features. Wall-washers provide a middle layer of lighting and beautiful silhouette effects. Underwater lighting is used for color, to project ripples on walls, and to light fountains and sculptures in pools and ponds."
James Sultan *Studio Lux*

→ Consider how your interior lighting scheme will appear from outside.

Designer	Crescent Lighting
Year	2000
Dimensions	Diam 5cm (1.95in)
Materials	Marine-grade stainless steel (or cast aluminum/brass); glass or polycarbonate cover

These neat little uplighters make use of LEDs and so have a long lamp life. Housing either four or 19 LEDs, in white or blue, the fittings can be used to mark the edge of driveways or steps, or utilized anywhere in an exterior space where small, low-maintenance lights are required.

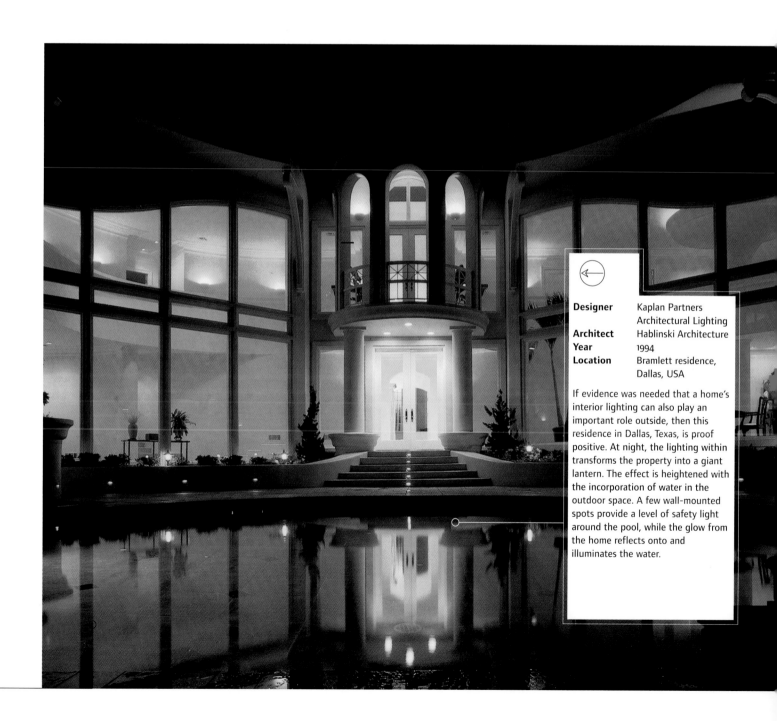

Designer Kaplan Partners
Architectural Lighting
Architect Hablinski Architecture
Year 1994
Location Bramlett residence,
Dallas, USA

If evidence was needed that a home's interior lighting can also play an important role outside, then this residence in Dallas, Texas, is proof positive. At night, the lighting within transforms the property into a giant lantern. The effect is heightened with the incorporation of water in the outdoor space. A few wall-mounted spots provide a level of safety light around the pool, while the glow from the home reflects onto and illuminates the water.

future highlights

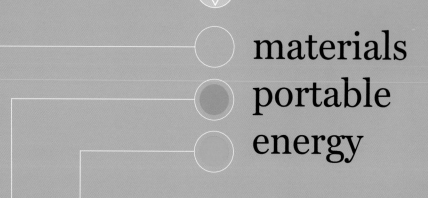

materials

portable

energy

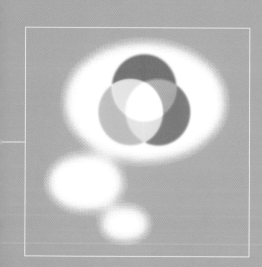

Future highlights:
Materials

The lighting sector makes use of a broad range of different materials. Lighting designers are producing pieces in which both the quality of the light emitted—whether it's ambient, accent, or colored—and the aesthetics of the fitting are equally important. Light fittings offered in a choice of materials allow you to select lighting that will coordinate with and complement other elements in an interior décor scheme.

If a room has been decorated in a particular color, for instance, it makes sense to incorporate light fittings that complement this color scheme. Likewise, certain materials work best with a particular theme. Minimalist interiors, for example, work well with industrial materials with sleek, clean lines.

Some materials that designers are currently fusing with light to wonderful effect are: glass, plastic, Perspex, ceramic, metal, rubber, paper, and wood. Each material has its own unique quality and interacts with light in a distinct way.

Year	Diffuse
Location	2000
Dimensions	H 25cm (9.75in), W 22cm (8.58in)
Materials	Porcelain

Cast in warm, translucent porcelain with a glowing silicon ring, Diffuse's Droplet range comprises a table light and pendant. The pendant (shown here), glowing with a warm pool of light spilling onto the floor below, can be used in a group or individually.

Designer	Modular Lighting Instruments
Year	2002
Dimensions	Various sizes available
Materials	Aluminum, polycarbonate

In Square Moon, polycarbonate has been used on either side of the light source to create a light filter. As these filters are supplied in different colors, the fittings can emit different hues of color as required. Square Moon is versatile, not only because of the color options, but also because it can be wall- or ceiling-mounted.

Glass

Glass has always had a crucial role to play in our homes, but recent years have seen architects and designers utilizing the material to a greater extent. Small glass windows are increasingly being replaced by floor-to-ceiling glazing—walls of glass that allow natural light to spill into a property by day and that transform the residence into a giant lantern by night, with the interior lighting glowing outward.

Of course, the use of glass isn't limited to a home's windows or walls. It can be used for tabletops, is ideal for shelving, and has always been a popular material for ornaments. Glass has a pure, clean look to it, as well as the ability to look delicate and fragile while actually being quite robust—toughened versions offer a more durable finish to work with and, crucially, a safer material should breakage occur.

Glass is also popular because of its translucency. Its ability to capture and also reflect light through its surface—whether natural or artificial light—makes it an excellent material choice, especially for designers whose work crosses the boundaries between light and art.

Glass looks stunning in its pure, clear form, but can also be etched—applying detailing to the glass surface, from intricate webbing through to crackled patterns, not only creates a more dynamic form, but also affects the way that light catches and shines from the glass piece.

The traditional chandelier—which fuses crystal glass and lighting to decorative effect—is finding many new, contemporary, and less stately forms, thanks to innovative modern designers (see pages 84–85).

Color can also transform glass, whether applied to the glass itself, or as a colored light source within the glass piece. LEDs are an ideal light source for this.

Designer	Greenapple
Year	2002
Dimensions	H 60cm (23.4in), W 14cm (5.46in), D 14cm
Materials	Glass

Greenapple's 712 lamp is an adaptation of the company's best-selling 705 lamp, a piece in which the wiring is rendered practically invisible by a clever design using four glass rods. The 712 lamp shares the same qualities as the 705, but is taller and, some might say, more elegant for its extra height.

Designer	Tom Dixon (available through Swarovski)
Manufacturer	Italamp Light Design Factory Srl
Distributor	Swarovski
Year	2003
Dimensions	H 100cm (39in), W 200cm (78in)
Materials	Swarovski crystal, nylon fibres

When world-famous designer Tom Dixon was briefed by Swarovski to use its crystal to create a modern twist on the traditional chandelier, he rose to the challenge admirably. Ball is a magical spherical piece for the digital age, making use of up-to-date LED technology.

Plastic

Plastic has often been derided as a cheap and tacky material, but it has been reclaimed by esteemed designers such as Verner Panton, Alessi, Philippe Starck, Ron Arad, and Karim Rashid. They have explored plastic's potential, using the material to create everything from smaller decorative accessories to larger furniture pieces. Their high-profile creations have helped to convince dubious designers that plastic—and its various derivatives, such as polypropylene, polyethylene, polycarbonate, and PVC—is an ideal material for product design. It is a flexible, easily moldable, durable, and lightweight material that lends itself to free-standing, portable pieces. It can also introduce a little much-needed color into domestic spaces. Such qualities, coupled with the crucial fact that plastic, like glass, offers a translucent medium through which light can shine, makes the material ideal for use in lighting as well as furniture design.

Verner Panton's 1970 Illumesa table could arguably be seen as one of the first forms to explore plastic's potential both in furniture and lighting design. Colored plastic was used to create the table's shell, while a standard lightbulb meant that the piece glowed from within with an inviting light. Decades after Illumesa, contemporary lighting designers are again playing with light sources within fittings or furniture made from colored plastic. When light travels through the colored skin, the effect can be magical. Of course, the reverse solution of utilizing colored lamps within translucent plastic can be equally effective.

Designer	Nick Crosbie for Inflate
Year	1996
Dimensions	H 15cm (5.85in), W 35cm (13.65in), D 35cm
Materials	PVC, polypropylene

With the name Inflate, it doesn't take too many guesses to work out what links all of the company's products—they're all inflatable. UFO (shown), Striplight, and Tablelight are three pieces that combine Inflate's trademark inflatable technique with lighting. All three come in frosted or clear color options and, thanks to the translucent materials from which they are made, light transmits throughout the funky fittings.

Designer	Verner Panton
Year	1970 (distributed by Louis Poulsen, Denmark); reissue in 1999 distributed by Innovation Randers, Denmark
Dimensions	H 36cm (14.04in), D 72cm (28.08in)
Materials	Vacuum-molded Cellidor

Created in the 1970s, Panton's Illumesa table—low enough for guests to sit around it on the floor—consists of two hollow plastic bodies (with the table surface slightly recessed), lit from within by a standard lightbulb. Initially available in red, orange, and violet, today it is only in produced in white and orange.

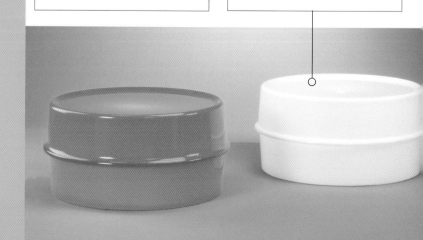

Designer	Modular Lighting Instruments
Year	2002
Dimensions	Various sizes available
Materials	Polycarbonate, steel

In Modular Lighting's Crosslink, polycarbonate has been used on either side of the light source to create a light filter. These filters are supplied in different colors, so the fittings can emit varying hues of color as required. Crosslink's modular structure means that each link can ultimately have a different colored filter attached—back or front— offering up endless combinations. As the piece can also be wall-mounted, several Crosslinks can be linked together to create a wall of light.

Perspex

Like plastic, Perspex has had a slightly rocky history in terms of its trend value. A few years back, the material was classed as kitsch, an outdated material choice generally associated with 1960s and 70s furniture. Perspex is no longer stuck in the past, however; it has been reconceived as a 21st-century material for adventurous, forward-thinking designers. Perspex has contemporary designers enthusing over the wonderful way that it interacts with light, the soft glow you can achieve through it, and the way it contains light and pushes it out of the edges.

Today, a band of designers is working almost exclusively with Perspex, attracted to the material specifically because of the way it transforms light. The fact that a sheet of Perspex carries and distributes a cool, even, light magically through and across its entire surface is an exciting proposition—especially when it comes to creating integrally lit furniture forms made from the material. With a wide palette of Perspex colors to choose from and an equally diverse selection of lighting options, there are seemingly no limits to the material's capabilities.

Some designers choose to create light fittings or furniture pieces made entirely out of Perspex, but a more subtle incorporation of the material, following a less-is-more design philosophy, can be just as effective. Complementary materials such as rich woods and leathers, in contrasting colors, can produce a stunning effect. Take an idea adopted by a number of designers, wherein tables or sofas are edge-lit using strips of Perspex to diffuse the light (see page 72).

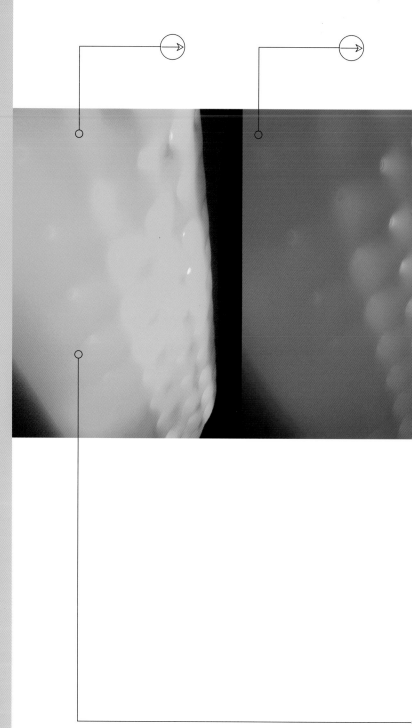

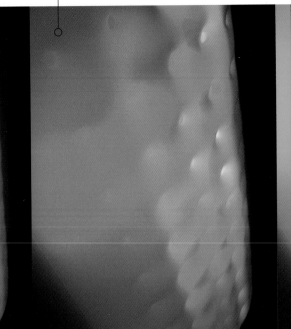

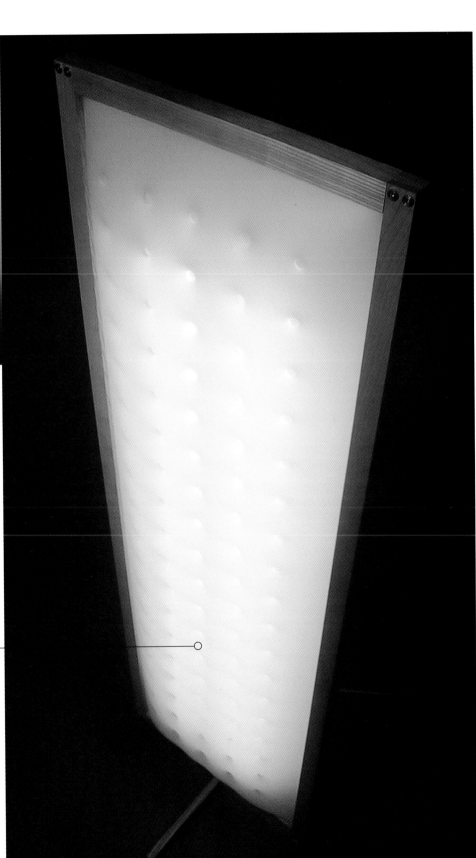

Designer	BoBo Design
Year	2000
Product	Prismex pillow
Dimensions	H 180cm (70.2in), W 54cm (21.06in)
Materials	Perspex
Photography	Nick Gant

The Perspex Pillow lighting panel makes use of Prismex ™, a Perspex sheet that creates a sculptural, soft, and tactile quality; and also carries and distributes a cool light through and across its entire surface. Color spectrum technology has been incorporated into the panel, allowing colors to change to suit the environment or mood.

Ceramic and porcelain

Ceramic and porcelain are materials that have been used for centuries, and have a timeless quality that continues to appeal to modern designers. These ancient materials can be given new life when handled in a contemporary manner. Though ceramics might be more commonly associated with decorative accessories and ornaments, they are equally viable when it comes to creating lighting. Whether they are used to form a base or to create the piece in its entirety, the result is ambient light emitting from a delicate-looking fitting with a sculptural element.

Many lighting designers working with ceramic or porcelain aim to extend the boundaries of these materials and apply them in product areas beyond the traditional uses for ceramic. But looking to the future doesn't necessarily mean disregarding how the materials have been used in the past. In fact, some of the most effective pieces fusing ceramic and porcelain with lighting are those where designers have taken the materials, handled them in time-honored traditions, using traditional craftsmanship, to create totally contemporary lighting forms.

Coupled with its ability to create an ambient glow, ceramics are famed for being one of the most durable finishes. They don't tarnish and won't degrade over time. They are also easy to clean and maintain. And, of course, pieces made from the material look equally beautiful when they are not illuminated.

Ceramic or porcelain lights are also extremely effective in exterior spaces. Light fittings made from ceramic or porcelain can perfectly complement the organic nature of a garden, are durable enough to withstand the elements, and can help create that must-have ambient glow to the space.

Designer **Diffuse**
Architect GA Design International and Sumisho Fine Goods Corporation
Year 2002
Location Portopia Hotel, Kobe, Japan

Diffuse was approached by architectural practice GA Design International and Sumisho Fine Goods Corporation to produce porcelain chandeliers for a hotel scheme that the practice was designing in Japan. Diffuse created 18 three-tiered chandeliers for the hotel's vast ballroom, each tier composed of individual, translucent porcelain pieces, slipcast to create texture. Using the same styling, Diffuse then went on to produce a series of tall porcelain wall sconces for the ballroom and lobby. The fact that the Portopia Hotel is situated in Japan, a well-known earthquake zone, threw up a major safety issue. Diffuse had to research a way of coating the porcelain with a safe, transparent material to sheathe it. A plastic laminate proved to be the perfect solution.

Designer Joanne Windaus for Mocha
Year 2002
Dimensions H 23cm (8.97in), Diam 12cm (4.68in)
Materials Unglazed porcelain

The Oz hanging light makes use of a material becoming increasingly popular in lighting design—porcelain. Designed to give a beautiful glow through its shade, almost like candlelight, each Oz Light is handmade and so unique in design.

Metal

Lighting designers have long used metallic finishes, but more often than not the look was industrial, tying in with minimalist interiors that were typified by chunks of steel and glass. While minimalism can still be an attractive proposition, the stark, industrial look so popular in city warehouse conversions has moved on, incorporating more human, personalized elements. In a world where injecting a sense of personality is as important as creating elegant, uncluttered spaces, neutral décors, and clean lines, interior elements such as lighting can help soften a room scheme, creating a sense of warmth.

Today, lighting designers are working with metal in a much "softer" way. The realization that metal, though a naturally hard material, can be relatively malleable, especially when heated, has opened up a world of possibilities. Metals such as aluminum and stainless steel are being twisted, bent, shaped, and sculpted to produce an array of different styles of luminaire, from simple cylindrical forms, highly polished to produce reflective surfaces, through to decorative forms where metal has been used in a sculptural way.

Whatever lighting form takes your fancy, you are guaranteed to have a fitting that will be extremely hardwearing, easy to maintain, and, crucially, will not date—some materials go in and out of fashion, but metal has been a constant.

Designer	The Bradley Collection
Year	1998
Dimensions	H 24cm (9.36in), L 24cm, W 10cm (3.9in)
Materials	Stainless steel

The Lobster Desk Light is one of a number of contemporary light fittings available from The Bradley Collection, all made from different types of metal. In this instance, stainless steel is shaped into a sleek design and topped off with a frosted glass visor. A wall sconce complements the desk light.

Designer	Ralph Ball for Ligne Roset
Location	2002
Dimensions	H 30cm (11.7in), Diam 29cm (11.31in)
Materials	Chromed metal

Ralph Ball's One Day is a table lamp in the shape of a trash can, supplied with ten sheets of drawings by the designer (the idea being that the owner screws these pieces of paper up and tosses them into the trash).

Rubber, wood, and paper

While glass, plastic, Perspex, ceramics, and metal are favorite materials for lighting designers, there remains a craving in the lighting design community—just as in the world of furniture and other product design—to explore the potential of other materials.

Rubber is a colorful, soft-to-the touch material that has attracted increasing interest in the design world in the past few years. Designers have been working with the material, exploiting its ability to be formed, cut, and woven into a plethora of shapes, to produce an array of products, including lighting.

Designers are also turning to natural materials for their lighting creations. Wood has long been used in furniture design, and lighting designers are increasingly recognizing that, with so many grades of wood to choose from, the material is ideal to use to create a shade for a light source, or indeed a fitting in its entirety. Having a luminaire made from wood also means that the lighting can have a stronger relationship with the interior as a whole, complementing other fixtures and fittings.

Paper is another rising star. Taking inspiration from the traditional, delicate beauty of Japanese lanterns, many designers are coming to appreciate that paper is an ideal material for creating cost-effective but sophisticated, and even sculptural, origami-like lightshades.

Designer	Ramon Valls for Taller Uno (distributed by Optelma)
Year	1995
Dimensions	H 26cm (10.14in), W 20cm (7.8in)
Materials	Multiply, pleated parchment

Vestal is a fine example of how using certain materials can produce fittings that have more of a 3D effect. Here the effect has been created through the use of pleated parchment for the fitting's shade.

Designer	Michel Tortel for Lucid Lighting, available through Atelier Sedap (distributed by Optelma)
Year	1999
Dimensions	H 24cm (9.36in), W 35cm (13.65in), D 13cm (5.07in)
Materials	Multiply, shaped wood

Cigale is a wall-mounted fixture that come in a choice of different wood finishes, ranging from light to dark. The piece demonstrates a particularly interesting use of the material: a circle of wood appears to have cracked open, revealing the light source within.

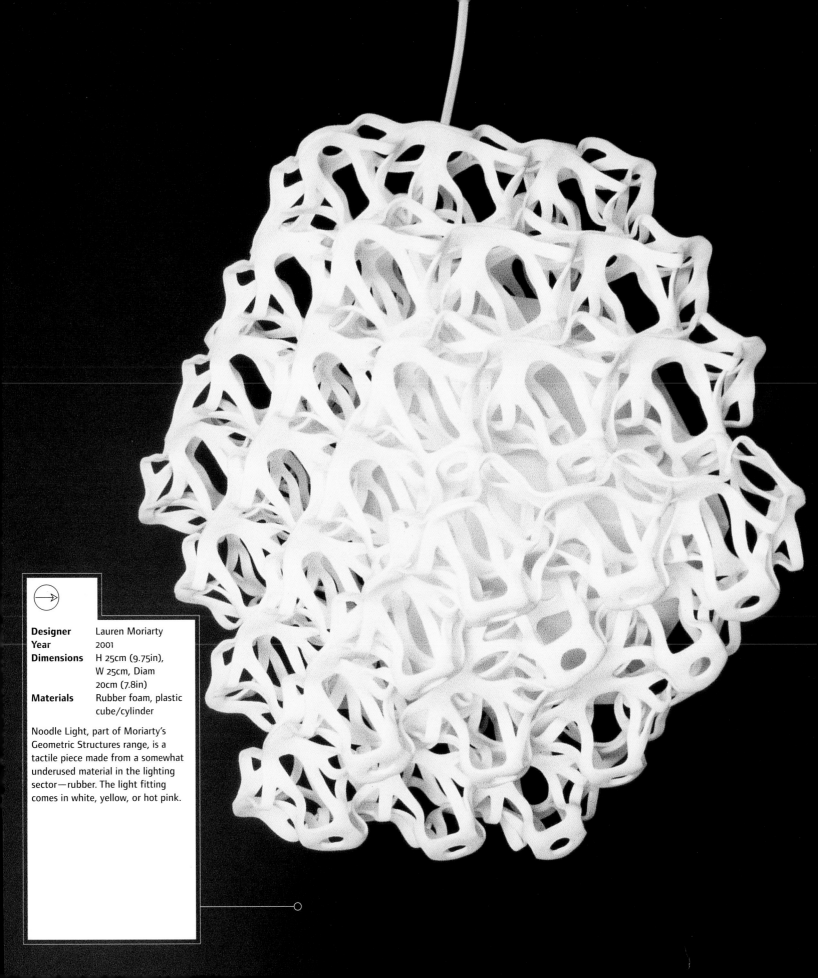

Designer Lauren Moriarty
Year 2001
Dimensions H 25cm (9.75in),
W 25cm, Diam
20cm (7.8in)
Materials Rubber foam, plastic
cube/cylinder

Noodle Light, part of Moriarty's
Geometric Structures range, is a
tactile piece made from a somewhat
underused material in the lighting
sector—rubber. The light fitting
comes in white, yellow, or hot pink.

Future highlights:
Portable

Wirefree technology is utilized in a number of domestic appliances—consider cordless phones or cell phones, which give us the freedom to talk while walking around. When we turn our attention to lighting, it's interesting to remember that the earliest sources of domestic lighting were completely portable. The light from oil lamps or candles would help guide people safely to their otherwise darkened sleeping quarters at night. When electric light came into use, it had many plus points, not least the fact that it offered a more constant source of light. But electric light meant incorporating wiring, which in turn meant that fittings had to be positioned in one particular place. In a world where we demand portability of our phones and computers, why shouldn't lighting follow suit? In the same way that other technologies used in the home have been freed from the shackles of wires, designers have begun experimenting with how lighting can become wirefree, no longer reliant on mains installation or plugging in.→

Designer   Alberto Meda
and Paolo Rizzatto
for Luceplan
Year   2002
Dimensions   H 31cm (12.09in),
Base 8cm^2 (3.12in^2)
Materials   Transparent or
metalized body

Billed as a 21st-century candle, STAR.LED is a completely portable fitting with not a wire in sight. Instead, the pretty table light—styled like a traditional candlestick—is lit by LED lighting technology, which is in turn powered by rechargeable batteries. The fitting is simply slotted into a transformer when the batteries need recharging.

One might assume that the only wirefree lighting solution is to revert back to fittings that accommodate candles or tea lights. While this is a pretty option, it is neither progressive nor sophisticated. The key is to create a fitting that can offer the constant light level that we're used to on the move. Many designers use the way that we charge our cell phones as inspiration: light fittings, whether handheld candles of the future or larger forms, are simply plugged into the mains to be charged. After an energy boost, they are disconnected and can operate as completely mobile lights. The use of rechargeable batteries further increases the lifespan of such lighting, before it has to be returned to its charger for reenergizing.

When it comes to which light sources to use in portable light fittings, there's a clear winner—LEDs. Small in size and therefore ideal for use in smaller pieces, LEDs also offer the potential for incorporating color. They are also one of the most energy-efficient light sources.

It would be wrong to say that the lighting market is swamped with portable lighting options—the creation of such lighting is still very much in its infancy. But that looks set to change, with many lighting designers looking at how their product portfolios can be enhanced with the introduction of wirefree pieces.→

Designer	Totem Design
Year	2001
Dimensions	H 37cm (14.43in), D 54cm (21.06in)
Materials	Polyethylene

Totem Design's boo! and bootoo! tap into the trend toward illuminated furniture that encourages interaction with the user. Boo! (shown here) automatically illuminates when sat upon and switches off when the user stands up. And when the multifunctional bootoo! is switched on and has its cushion removed, the owner has an illuminated table, or indeed a funky light. While the products, which come in a host of bright colors, do rely on plugging in, their lightweight structure means that they're not limited to positioning in one particular place.

Many lighting designers are keen to address the portability issue, especially with regard to outdoor lighting, where the opportunity to move lighting around the exterior space has obvious benefits. It is, of course, possible to treat smaller items—pendants, table, and floor lights—designed for interior use, as a middle ground between fixed and portable, because they are so lightweight. Rooms in homes frequently have a number of plug sockets dotted around the space. A lightweight piece—made from featherweight materials such as polycarbonate or PVC—can be moved around with ease.

When it comes to outdoor portable lighting, there is another option—solar power. No wiring is required, and there is no need to recharge by plugging in. The sun is the energy source. Combine a lightweight material with solar power, and you're onto a sustainable winning formula.

While it's obvious that permanently fixed lighting will always have its place in the home, portable fittings are an exciting development. Their emergence signals a growing awareness that lighting can be interactive to a greater degree. We like to rearrange rooms in our homes, trying out new furniture layouts. Why not reposition our lighting in different places, too, to stimulate different functions and moods?

Designer BoBo Design
Year 2001
Dimensions H 75cm (29.25in),
W 220cm (85.8in)
Materials Perspex
Photography Nick Gant

Designed by BoBo's directors Nick Gant and Tanya Dean, these lightweight Perspex forms can be used in a multitude of ways: as interior lighting, seating, or storage; or as exterior illumination or furniture. The Glonuts, which come in numerous colors, can be wall- or floor-mounted, or stacked up to create a unique lighting installation.

Designer Mathmos
Year 2002
Dimensions L 13cm (5.07in),
H 9cm (3.51in)
Materials Polished die-cast zinc, soft-touch thermoplastic, silicone

Fun, interactivity, and portability are three concepts that underpin Mathmos's Mobiles range. Such qualities are clearly embodied in Aduki, a colorful little fitting that can be used indoors or out, and either hung as a pendant or laid flat. As with other pieces in the Mobiles range, Aduki doesn't just emit white light, but can move through the color spectrum or be frozen on one hue.

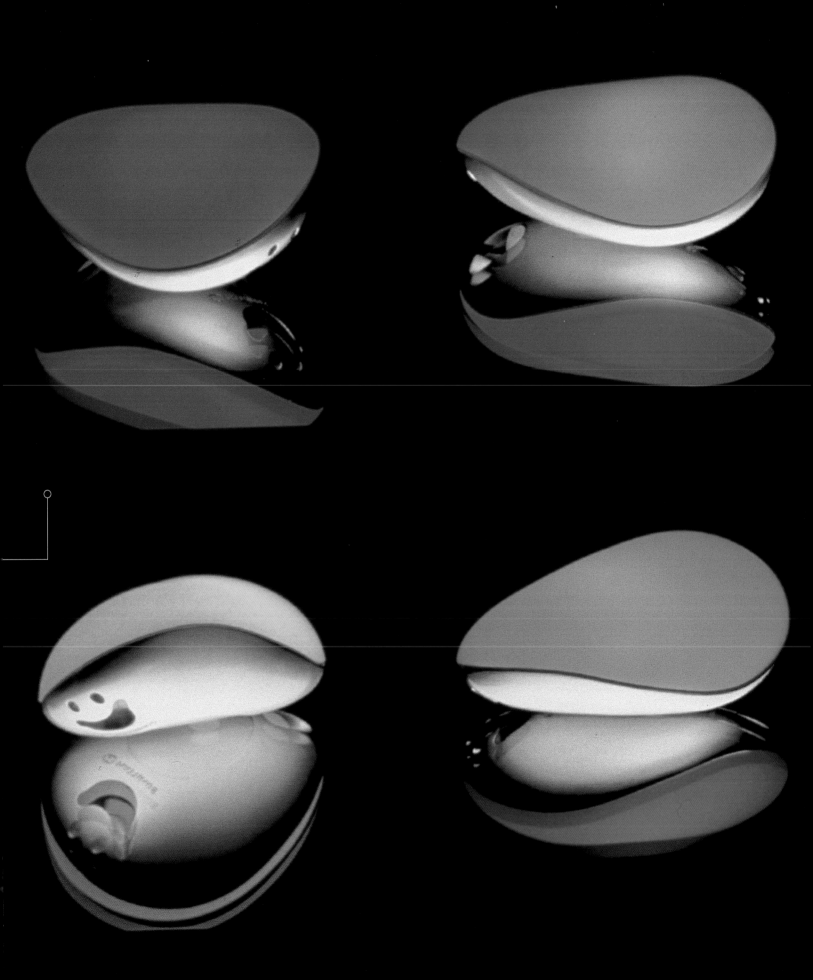

Spotlight on:
Mathmos

Mathmos, the company behind the original lava lamps of the 1960s, is a firm that leads the way when it comes to portable lighting. Mathmos's managing director, Cressida Granger, says: "Phones and computers are so much better wirefree, so why not lights?"

The Mathmos Mobiles collection responds to this—the lights are chargeable in the same way as cell phones, and there are no bulbs or batteries to replace as each piece makes use of LEDs.

With all of Mathmos's lighting products, interactivity is key. Consider the firm's seminal lava lamps: wax inside the lamps rises when warmed, creating a traveling light effect that has inspired generations of students' lucid experiences. Playful mobile pieces take this interactivity one step further, inviting physical interaction.

Tumbler Flip is a piece that exemplifies this playfulness. "It is important to us that the way the products work is magical, and that their interactivity reveals itself over time. With Tumbler, firstly you realize that it changes color, then that it is the movement of the object that changes the color, on what facets you can achieve which color, and how to turn it on and off. You can also experiment with placement for the product around the house and garden."

Color change is a crucial component, whether the piece is flipped to shift color or switched to "Faze" mode, wherein the piece works automatically through the different color options. Aduki, a handheld mobile (see pages 100 and 132), works on a similar principle. It can be laid on a flat surface or hung up, and either moves through different colorways—red to green, blue to red, and green to blue—or can be frozen on a desired color. Bubble, a silicone ball of light, comes with an optional nest for sitting in which also changes color.

When one considers that Tumbler and Bubble provide an average of three to six hours of light per charge, and that they incorporate a rechargeable battery that will power more than 1,000 charges, Mathmos is perhaps right to refer to such products as the candles of the future.

Highlights

○ Use portable lighting for interior and exterior spaces. If color-changing properties are built into portable light fittings, choose a color that suits the mood.

○ Use a number of portable light fittings to create an interesting light installation. Mathmos's Tumbler blocks can be put together to create a color-changing wall of light.

Designer	Mathmos
Year	2000
Dimensions	Diam 8cm (3.12in)
Materials	Silicone

What else could Mathmos call this cute ball of light but Bubble? Lit by LEDs and, like other pieces in the Mathmos Mobiles range, designed for use both indoors and out, the fully rechargeable, playful light doesn't emit just one tint but changes color. The piece comes with its own holder, the Bubble Nest, allowing it to be hung on a wall or placed on a surface with or without the charger lead.

Designer	Mathmos
Year	2001
Dimensions	H 10cm (3.9in),
	L 18cm (7.02in),
	D 6cm (2.34in)
Materials	Glass

Why have one color option when you can have a piece that changes color? That was the thinking behind Mathmos's Tumbler Flip, another product in the company's Mathmos Mobiles range. Tumbler Flip is a rechargeable glass block that changes color when it is turned on its side. Keep flipping it and the piece works its way through nine color options. As there are no wires (the piece utilizes LEDs), Tumbler Flip can be used indoors and out.

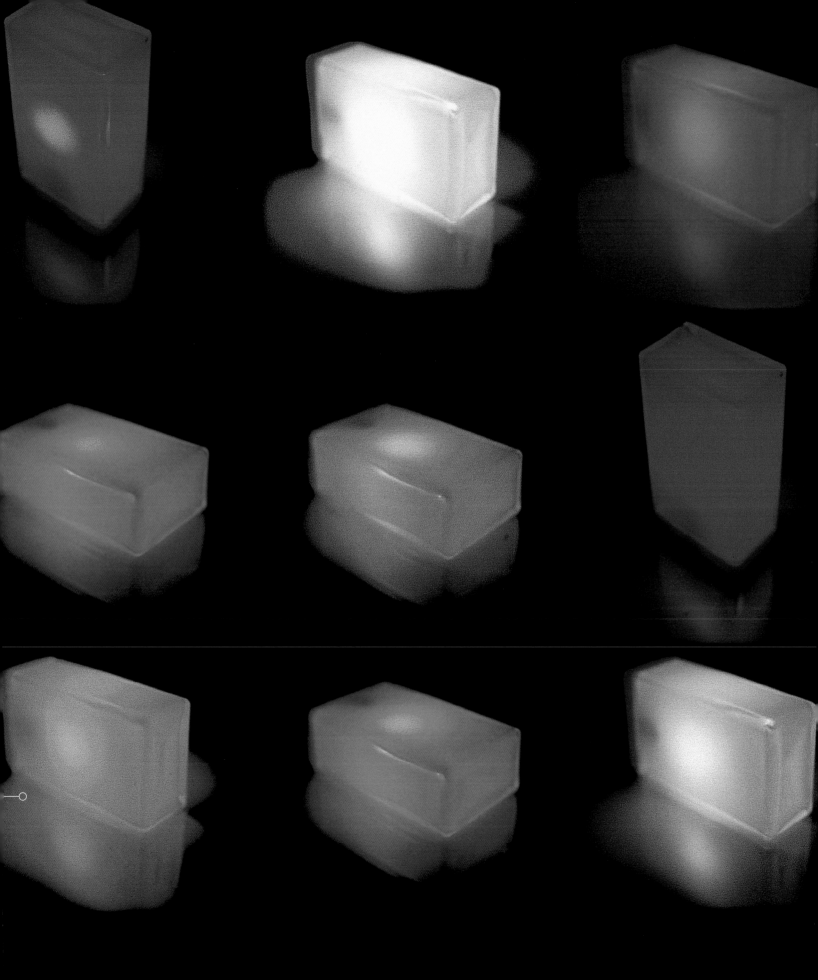

Future highlights:
Energy

For all its many attributes, lighting has one serious failing. If we consider just how much lighting our homes incorporate, and add up how many fixtures and fittings we have in each room, then that downside is obvious: collectively, we are using up a lot of electricity.

We are all being encouraged to be more environmentally aware, and energy-efficiency has become a buzz term. Domestic appliances such as washing machines are now being designed to be less wasteful of electricity, and it follows that lighting can also be designed with greater energy-efficiency in mind.

Organizations dedicated to promoting energy-saving practices are armed with some telling facts and figures. Consider, for instance, that lighting typically accounts for up to 30 percent of a household's total electricity costs. Furthermore, only 10 percent of the energy that lighting consumes is used to provide the actual light; the remainder is emitted as unwanted and unnecessary heat.

The Energy Saving Trust, a UK-based organization, makes an interesting point: if every UK household installed just three compact fluorescent lamps—the most energy-efficient light sources—enough energy would be saved in a year to power the country's street lighting grid. While compelling statistics such as this should be encouragement enough, there has—and to some extent remains—a stumbling block: energy-efficient bulbs invariably come at a higher price compared to standard-wattage light sources. There is a simple counter-argument to this, however, but it requires homeowners to think long-term. Energy-efficient light sources might cost more than standard-wattage bulbs initially, but they are capable of lasting ten times longer. There is less need, then, to replace bulbs so frequently. And it is not just about saving money: bulbs that use less energy also help reduce electricity charges— energy-efficient lightbulbs typically reduce energy consumption by as much as 70 percent due to their low wattage.→

Designer   Bushe Associates
Year   2001
Location   Prince Bar, London, UK
Photography   Paul Tyagi/View

The lighting in this bar is a shining example of how designers can work with energy-efficient lighting to create exciting and innovative lighting schemes. Low-energy light sources have been used throughout the bar, often in a discreet way so that, while the fitting can't be seen, the lighting effect can. In the washroom, low-energy lamps have been recessed into the pelmet. Low-voltage lamps have also been used to make a feature of the bottle display that stretches from the bar into the restaurant. Here, low-voltage lamps on stalks have been inserted into empty bottles among the wine-bottle display.

When energy-efficient lighting first reached public consciousness, the concept seemed to jump ahead of the light fittings sector. Oversized bulbs, many of which couldn't even be accommodated into fittings, seemed to be the only option. But lighting manufacturers have turned this situation around, introducing stylish fittings designed for use with energy-efficient light sources. Such sources include the likes of compact fluorescent lamps and low-voltage bulbs, allowing for good-looking, cost- and energy-effective pieces.

Isometrix Lighting + Design's color-changing system, Colourwash (see pages 64–67), is a good example. When the company was designing this intelligent system, the timing was perfect to make use of an energy-efficient light source. As lighting product designer Chris Miller says: "The emergence of low-voltage halogen lamps helped Isometrix to develop the product, concurrent with the public's acceptance of low-voltage lights as an energy-saving alternative to standard bulbs."

Low-voltage halogen might have been Isometrix's energy-efficient lighting of choice, but when a more discreet source is required, LEDs are ideal. Low-wattage, low-voltage, emitting very little heat, and offering up to 100,000 hours lifetime, LEDs are a feasible and attractive alternative to traditional light sources. They're fantastic because of their long life and cool running, there's excellent energy-efficiency, and their longevity reduces maintenance costs.→

Designer Arc Lighting
Year 2001
Dimensions H 15cm^2 (5.85in^2)
Materials Glass
Photography Holly Jolliffe

Pure Colour, a range of illuminated tiles designed by Arc Lighting for use inside and outside the home (see page 70), highlights the fact that good-looking lighting solutions can also be energy-efficient. The tiles, offered in a host of colors and sizes, with the choice of sandblasted perimeters (Pure Colour Mirror) and color-changing lighting (Pure Colour Chroma), are illuminated using LEDs—one of the most energy-efficient sources currently available. The products have an average lamp life of some 40,000 hours, generate hardly any heat, and consume only one watt of power.

Energy-efficiency isn't the sole reserve of particular light sources. Effective lighting design should use the most energy-efficient fixture that is best suited for each illuminated task. That means not only making the most of compact fluorescents and other low-wattage light sources, but also using dimming switches and systems—either local or "total home." These provide one-touch control for scenes, pathways, multiple functions (lights on, shades lowered, etc), and can reduce energy consumption considerably.

Lighting control systems incorporating dimmers can be a great way of establishing energy-efficient lighting throughout a home. Some of the more sophisticated systems also incorporate occupancy detection, which work in response to motion, with infrared sensors detecting body heat. By installing occupancy sensors on ceilings or walls, lighting comes on or off depending on whether infrared radiation is detected, and thus can help reduce lighting bills and cut energy costs.→

Designer	C + B Lefebvre for Ligne Roset
Year	2002
Dimensions	Floor lamp H 190cm (74.1in, vertical) or 173.7cm (67.74in, horizontal), W 25cm (9.75in), D 25cm
Materials	Aluminum

LD1, a range comprising a wall light and a floor standard lamp, is proof positive that energy-efficient light sources can be put to use in a host of light fittings. In this instance, LEDs (117 in total) are used to provide a level of light equivalent to a normal-wattage light source, while using less energy and giving off minimal heat. The floor standard lamp is equipped with a dimmer, allowing the user to reduce the level of light to create a more ambient glow.

Designer	Arc Lighting
Year	System Tread 1999; System Tread Colour 2001; System Muro 2002
Dimensions	System Tread: H 100cm (39in), W 60cm (23.4in), D 8.5cm (3.32in); System Tread Colour: H 120cm (46.8in), W 60cm (23.5in), D 8.5cm (3.32in); System Muro H 100cm (39in), W 50cm (19.5in), D 7.6cm (2.96in)
Materials	Glass
Photography	Holly Jolliffe

System Tread is a fluorescent, illuminated glass floor. System Muro allows you to inset individual lightboxes into the wall.

Fixtures and fittings incorporating low-voltage, low-wattage light sources meet the demand for energy-efficient lighting but, as some designers are asserting, it is equally possible to fuse energy-efficient lighting with environmentally friendly materials. Many contemporary table lamps, wall lights, pendants, and chandeliers use compact, fluorescent, tungsten bulbs and low-voltage light sources. Furthermore, many designers are defying modern "throwaway society", by using durable or recycled materials in combination with more efficient light sources.

Lighting might not be the only guilty party when it comes to energy wastage, but it is certainly something that can be designed with energy and environmental conservation in mind. When these properties are combined with functional and aesthetic attributes, beautiful, energy-efficient domestic lighting is accessible to all of us.

Designer Ross Lovegrove for Luceplan
Year 1998
Dimensions H 37cm (14.43in), W 15cm (5.85in)
Materials Aluminum stem, transparent polycarbonate head

Ross Lovegrove's energy-efficient Solar Bud lights collect solar energy via a polycrystalline silicon photovoltaic cell that powers rechargeable batteries. In the absence of light, an electronic circuit pilot automatically turns on three high-efficiency red LEDs in the fitting's head.

Designer Light & Design Associates & DTZ
Supplier Arc Lighting
Year 2002
Location Lancashire Court, UK
Photography Holly Jolliffe

Arc Lighting's Pure Colour range of vividly colored illuminated tiles has been designed with versatility of use in mind and can, thus, be used virtually anywhere—indoors or out. Light & Design Associates & DTZ made innovative use of Arc's Pure Colour Pavia to transform a simple sidewalk. As the tiles are water-resistant and make use of energy-efficient LEDs (which last a lot longer than traditional light sources), Pure Colour is ideal for such hardwearing applications.

Spotlight on:
Lighting Research Center

The New York-based Lighting Research Center (LRC) collaborated with the US Environmental Protection Agency (US EPA) on the Saratoga Energy-Efficient Home—an initiative that demonstrates the attraction and cost-effectiveness of energy-efficient lighting solutions.

LRC incorporated concealed lighting, to show how energy-efficient lighting can be used to create an ambient effect, where the wash of light, as opposed to the fitting, is seen. Making use of the new, improved linear fluorescents, which are available with electronic ballasts, in a wide range of wattages, lengths, and even dimming capabilities, hidden lighting was applied in a number of ways, often integrated into the architectural elements throughout the home. Coves and valances proved particularly good hiding spots, great for providing uniform lighting and adding interest to the interior spaces.

In the dining room, project manager Patricia Rizzo explains: "A cove was mounted above the decorative columns and appeared to extend from the columns themselves." LEDs, versatile not least because of their small size, inject colored ambient light. "Amber LEDs were inserted in the glass transom above the door leading into the study. They were invisible to the eye, and edge-lit the seeded glass to create a warm, inviting glow."

Accent lighting was chosen to highlight artwork. "Low-voltage halogen lamps (MR16s) were used because they are available in such a variety of beam spreads that one can accent a sculpture or painting as narrowly or widely as one wishes without having light spill over."

While the permanent accent and ambient lighting was created by the LRC designers, when it came to free-standing and decorative light fittings, the owners were given a choice of fittings which could incorporate energy-efficient lightbulbs, or make use of compact fluorescent lamps.

Energy-efficiency isn't wasted through lighting being turned on in unoccupied rooms, so LRC installed occupancy sensors, activated by infrared or ultrasonic wavelengths. These detect motion or body heat at various ranges and activate a light source only when the space is occupied. The sensors can be programmed so that they turn off a certain time after a person leaves the room.

The layered lighting effect achieved in this property—ambient, accent, and decorative—is testimony to the fact that energy-efficient lighting is a viable choice for every facet of a home's lighting scheme.

Lighting Designer	Jean Paul Freyssinier-Nova and Patricia Rizzo, in collaboration with the US EPA
Year	2002
Location	Saratoga Energy-Efficient Home, Saratoga Springs, USA
Donor Manufacturers	Advance Transformer Co, Alkco, Bartco Lighting, GE Lighting, Lightolier, Lutron, OSRAM SYLVANIA, Philips Lighting, Prescolite, Sea Gull Lighting, The Watt Stopper, Westinghouse Lighting Corp, Energy Saving Ballasts
Supporting Manufacturers	Dreamscape, Kichler
Builder	Belmonte Builders, Clifton Park, New York
Photography	Michael Kalla

The design of the exterior fixtures lent themselves to incandescent bulbs, so low wattages (25 watts) were used to minimize glare.

Highlights

○ Use occupancy detectors to avoid wasting light when it doesn't need to be on.

○ Incorporate dimmers so that levels of light can be easily adjusted.

○ Conceal linear fluorescents in ceiling coves or valances to create a hidden wash of ambient light.

The hallway

Hidden and visible lighting fuse to create a warm, energy-efficient glow. The hidden light comes by way of miniature fluorescent fixtures, concealed in symmetrical ceiling coves that flank the entry to the sunroom/hallway.

The bathroom

Bathrooms, especially vanity areas, need to fuse functional and aesthetic lighting. In the vanity area here, low-wattage linear fluorescents cast light evenly downward, softened by a diffuser, which helps to eliminate any shadowing caused by poorly direct light.

The master bedroom

A clean, tranquil effect was achieved in this room by making the entire wall a light source, through the use of concealed valance linear fluorescent strip lights. As these are dimmable, the homeowner can create different lighting moods. Compact fluorescent lamps have also been incorporated into the table lamps to cast a soft glow. The walk-in closet is lit by a surface-mounted fixture, containing three compact fluorescent lamps. A wall-switch occupancy sensor helps save energy by turning off the lights when there is no one in the room.

Trade secrets

→ Energy-efficient lighting can be used in many imaginative ways, just like traditional sources; linear sources can easily be concealed, especially with new, slimmer profiles.

"Think about energy-efficiency in terms of power usage, maintenance, life, and heat, and use available specialist lighting accordingly. And don't be put off by higher initial installation and product costs."
Phil Riley *The Light Lab*

→ "LED lighting is a light for the future in every sense, with low-heat emission so little energy wasted, and over 100,000 hours life span in comparison with 1,000 to 2,000 hours of normal bulbs."
Karin Sanner *Global Glass Art*

→ "Dimming systems are a fundamental source of energy savings in residential projects where color of light and color rendering are so critical."
Dave McCarroll *Kaplan Partners Architectural Lighting*

→ "A lighting control system can set the light levels to increase gradually throughout the day, reacting to the sun's strength and thus saving energy."
Chris Miller *Isometrix Lighting + Design*

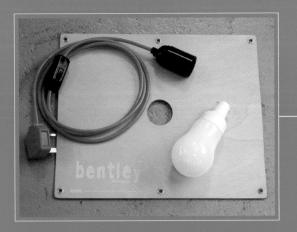

Designer Splinter Products
Year 2000
Dimensions L 34cm (13.26in),
W 29cm (11.31in)
D 0.8cm (0.31in)
x 2 sheets
Materials Birch ply

The Bentley luminaire by Splinter is
a self-assembly flat-pack lamp
specifically designed for use with
low-heat emission compact
fluorescent lamps. By sliding the
lamp and lampholder between two
sheets of birch ply, a fitting that can
be either hung, sat on the floor, or
wall-mounted, is created. Two
versions are offered: Bentley Basic
and Bentley Original. The front panel
of the former comes in standard
white, while the latter comes in a
choice of four colors: white, blue,
pink, or red.

appendix

Glossary

Accent lighting—lighting focused on a particular object or feature, sometimes referred to as directional light, and frequently achieved through the use of spotlights

Ambient lighting—lighting, often indirect and therefore hidden from view, used to create a soft, inviting glow in a room

Backlight—illumination from behind, and often above, an area or object, highlighting its edge and creating a separation between subject and background

Ballast—an electronic device used with fluorescent, mercury vapour, high- and low-pressure sodium or metal halide lamps to ensure that the proper amount of power is provided for starting and operating the lamp. It also stabilizes the current, regulating the pace of electric flow after start-up to ensure continued, safe operation

Bollard—an outdoor, upright, ground-mounted unit typically used to light walkways, steps, or other pathways

Bulb—a decorative glass or plastic housing that diffuses the light distribution. Also the layperson's term for lamp

Compact fluorescent lamp—often abbreviated to CFL and also referred to as PL, Twin-Tube or BIAX lamps. Offers a lamp life about ten times that of incandescent lamps and uses less power, making it an energy-efficient option

Cold cathode—a form of fluorescent lighting that can be sized and shaped to conform to any architectural space, with an extremely long lamp life (some 50,000 hours)

Color filter—the main method for producing colored light, the filter used in conjunction with a "white" light source

Cornice lighting—a lighting system comprising light sources shielded by a panel parallel to the wall and attached to the ceiling that distributes light over the wall

Cove lighting—a system in which light sources are shielded by a ledge or recess, to distribute light over the ceiling and upper wall

Dichroic filter—taken from the Greek word meaning "two-color," the filter achieves a rich, saturated color without actually using any colored materials. One color, or a broad range, is reflected or cancelled out, while another color, or a narrow range of colors, is transmitted through the filter itself

Diffuser—a translucent piece of glass or plastic that shields the light source in a fixture and distributes light in an even, soft, or scattered manner

Dimmer—device that through the use of a switch, knob, or slide lever changes the intensity of light by regulating electrical power delivered to the lamp

Direct lighting—a term that generally describes the installation of ceiling-mounted or suspended luminaires with mostly downward light distribution

Downlighter—a luminaire that directs light downward

Electronic ballasts—use of these lightweight ballasts allows the lamp to start instantly, thereby consuming significantly less energy

Energy-saving lamp—a lamp type designed with more efficient operation in mind, operating at a lower wattage than a standard lamp

Filament—a thin wire in a lightbulb that emits light when heated by an electric current

Fixture—the components that make up the complete housing of a light fitting

General lighting—the illumination of a large area

Glare—uncontrolled light that produces discomfort to the viewer

Floor lamp—a freestanding upright lamp for positioning on the floor

Fluorescent—a linear, energy-efficient light source consisting of a tube filled with inert gases. Light is emitted when an electric current is passed through it

Halogen—very low-wattage lamps that employ a halogen-gas additive to improve lamp life and efficacy. High-intensity light is generated through a combination of specially coated, highly efficient reflectors

HID—High-Intensity Discharge, a type of lamp

Housing—the body of a fixture

Incandescent—an incandescent lamp, also known as a filament lamp, produces light when its wire filament, made of tungsten, is heated by electricity to incandescence. Various sizes, wattages, and shapes, in clear, frosted, or white-coated bulbs are available

Indirect lighting—lighting in which luminaires are ceiling-suspended or wall-mounted, distributing light upward so it is reflected off the ceiling or walls

Lamp—what the lighting industry technically calls a lightbulb. Also used to describe the actual source of light in a fixture, i.e. halogen lamp

Lamp life—a lamp's average lifespan measured in hours

Lampshade—an opaque or translucent covering added to fittings to enhance their appearance and also shield the light source and/or direct the light

LED (Light Emitting Diode)—a small, low-voltage light source, which lights up when current flows through it

(A)

LENS—a diffuser for a light fixture, normally made of glass or plastic

Light pollution—lighting distributed in outdoor areas where it is not desired and cannot be utilized

Localized lighting—lighting designed to illuminate a specific area, such as a work area

Louver—a metal or plastic accessory used to prevent glare, whether it is absorbing or blocking unwanted light, or reflecting or redirecting light

Low-voltage lighting—a lamp/system that uses less than a 50-volt current (commonly 6, 12, or 24 volts). A transformer is used to convert the 120 volt to a lower voltage

Lumen—a measure of the amount of light produced by a lamp; the light emitted

Luminance—the amount of light reflected or transmitted by a light source

Luminaire—the technical term for a light fixture; the complete lighting unit

Luminous intensity—the amount of light emitted in a certain direction

Lux (LX)—a metric unit used to measure the illuminance of a surface

Metal halide—a high-intensity discharge (HID) lamp in which the major portion of the light is produced by radiation of metal halides, argon, and mercury vapours

Occupancy sensor—a control device that acts as a light switch upon sensing that a person has entered a space

Pendant—lighting that is suspended from the ceiling

Recessed luminaire—luminaire mounted above the ceiling, behind a wall, or other surface so that the projected light takes prominence

Reflector—the part of the luminaire that reflects light (usually downward)

Solar electricity—electricity generated by the sun

Solar energy—energy received from the sun

Spotlight—a small fitting projecting concentrated light

Strip fixture—a fluorescent fixture composed of only a channel to hold the ballast and sockets

T8/T12 lamp—industry-standard fluorescent lamps

Table lamp—a freestanding lamp placed on a table or nightstand

Task lighting—lighting directed to a specific worksurface or area

Track lighting—luminaires attached to a recessed or suspended linear track system, used for accent and general lighting applications

Transformer—electrical devices with no moving parts that change distribution voltages to higher or lower levels

Tungsten halogen—the classic household lightbulb, comprising a tungsten filament incandescent lamp filled with halogen gas, and a lamp envelope made of quartz to withstand the high temperature

Voltage—the measurement of electrical potential

Wall sconce—a decorative and functional wall-mounted luminaire

Wall-washer—term used to describe lighting illuminating vertical surfaces from ceiling to floor

Warm-up time—lighting term referring to the amount of time from turn-on to 90 percent light output

Watt (W)—internationally accepted measurement of the electrical power required by a product to operate; the power going in the lamp

Addresses

Professional Associations/Lighting Bodies

American Lighting Association
Trade association for manufacturers and distributors of residential lighting products in the USA and Canada.
www.americanlightingassoc.com
T. 00 1 800 274 4484

The Association of Lighting Designers (ALD)
Professional body representing lighting designers in all fields in the United Kingdom and the rest of the world.
www.ald.org.uk
T. 44 (0) 1707 891848

International Association for Energy-Efficient Lighting (IAEEL)
A global contact network and information resource for energy-efficient lighting.
www.iaeel.org

International Association of Lighting Designers
Chicago-based association providing education and networking for architectural lighting designers.
www.iald.org
T. 00 1 312 527 3677

International Commission on Illumination (CIE)
An organization devoted to international cooperation and exchange of information among its member countries on all matters relating to the science and art of lighting.
www.cie.co.at
T. 43 1 714 31 87 0

The Lighting Association
The largest organization in Europe for lighting companies and professionals.
www.lightingassociation.com
T. 44 (0) 1952 290905

National Lighting Bureau (NLB)
A nonprofit, industry-sponsored USA lighting information source, focusing on the quality of lighting.
www.nlb.org
T. 00 1 301 587 9572

Society of Light and Lighting
The professional body for lighting in the UK, with more than 2,100 members in the UK and worldwide.
www.cibse.org
T. 44 (0) 20 8772 3622

Lighting—General Information

Decorating etc Inc
A large selection of discount lighting from major manufacturers, including chandeliers, wall sconces, bathroom lighting, pendants, landscape lighting, table, desk and floor lamps, and ceiling fans.
www.decorating-etc.com

Elumit
A lighting search engine created by and for lighting specifiers, featuring some 12,000 lighting products from 25 lighting manufacturers.
www.eLumit.com

Lightforum.com
A leading source for information in the field of architectural lighting, operated by *Architectural Lighting Magazine.*
www.lightforum.com

LightingDirectory.com
Commercial lighting companies—predominantly from the UK—promote their products and services on this website.
www.lightingdirectory.com

Lightinglinx.com
Internet search engine for lighting designers.
www.lighting-linx.com

Lighting Research Center
Part of Rensselaer Polytechnic Institute, the Lighting Research Center is the leading university-based research center devoted to lighting, investigating lighting issues, and educating the next generation of lighting leaders.
www.lrc.rpi.edu
T. 00 1 518 687 7100

The Lighting Resource
Minneapolis-run website dedicated to lighting.
www.lightresource.com

Lightsearch.com
An internet resource for lighting specifiers and buyers.
www.lightsearch.com
T. 00 1 541 344 1909

Outdoor Lighting Directory
Website dedicated to manufacturers and distributors who specialize in outdoor lighting.
www.outdoor-lighting-directory.com

Searchspec
Search engine aimed at lighting professionals and specifiers, providing access to new solutions, suppliers, and thousands of products.
www.searchspec.com

Lighting Magazines

Architectural Lighting Magazine
Published seven issues a year and reaches 25,000 lighting designers, architects, interior designers, and engineers who specify for both commercial and residential projects.
www.archlighting.com

Flare
Italian architectural lighting magazine.
http://flare1.com

Home Lighting & Accessories
American trade magazine for the decorative lighting industry, read by retailers, distributors, manufacturers, architects, designers, and other lighting professionals.
www.homelighting.com

Licht
German magazine for lighting technicians, engineers, and designers.
www.pflaum.de

Light & Lighting
UK-based magazine covering design projects and the entire spectrum of lighting technology.
www.building.co.uk

Light Magazine
Trade magazine from British publisher ETP that focuses primarily on the retail and contract markets.
www.design4design.com

Lighting Equipment News
British trade publication, highlighting news in the lighting industry.
www.emap.com

Lighting Journal
Produced by the Institute of Lighting Engineers in the UK, the title focuses on the art and science of lighting.
www.ile.co.uk

Residential Lighting Magazine
One of the titles from the Décor Division of Illinois-based Vance Publishing Corp, which publishes several of the USA's home furnishing industry's leading business-to-business magazines. Emerging trends, innovative styles, and new products are showcased.
www.residentiallighting.com

Lighting Exhibitions

100% Design
One of the leading interior events, held in London and showcasing the full spectrum of design, including lighting. This is a trade event, but the public are welcome on one day.
www.100percentdesign.co.uk

Fiam
International Valencia-based fair dedicated to lighting fixtures, accessories, and components.

Ineltec
Three-part exhibition held in Basel, Switzerland, one section of which is dedicated to light and lighting technology.
www.ineltec.ch

Intel
Exhibition of electrical technology and electronics, with a lighting exhibition called World Light Show held within.
www.intelshow.com

International Contemporary Furniture Fair (ICFF)
New York plays host to a major furniture fair, showcasing the best product design—including lighting—from around the world.
www.icff.com

Light
Biannual trade exhibition for lighting professionals, and professional electricity and teletechnics for buildings, held in Helsinki, Finland.
www.finnexpo.fi

The Lighting Show
Co-located with three other events—The Furniture Show, Furnishing Accessories, and Design Interiors—and an additional three on a biannual basis—KBB, Expotile, and Soft Furnishings—The Lighting Show is the UK's only dedicated trade exhibition for the domestic and contract decorative lighting markets.
www.thefurnitureshow.co.uk

Pragointerier New Design
International professional fair of furniture, interior design, lighting, domestic textiles, and interior accessories.
www.incheba.cz/pragointerier

Scandinavian Furniture Fair
Trade exhibition with a special Accessories and Design section that includes lighting. Members of the public can attend the event on its public day.
www.scandinavianfurniturefair.com

Total Lighting at Interbuild
Trade exhibition held every two years, in the UK, that comprises a number of stand-alone exhibitions, including Total Lighting, an event that brings together suppliers of lighting equipment, products, and services with buyers and specifiers.
www.interbuild.com

Lightfair International (LFI)
Annual architectural and commercial lighting trade show and conference, held in New York.
www.lightfair.com
www.feriavalencia.com

Featured designers

AJ Browne and Co
T. +44 (0) 207 724 8280
www.ajbrowne.com

Arc Lighting
T. +44 (0) 1983 523399
www.arclighting.com

Artemide
T. +44 (0) 20 7631 5200
www.artemide.com

Ben Rousseau
T. +44 (0) 7980 843768
www.benrousseau.co.uk

Blue Beacon Lighting
T. +44 (0) 870 241 3992
www.bluebeacon.co.uk

Bruce Munro
T. +44 (0) 1749 813 898
www.brucemunro.co.uk

Bruce Oldfield
T. +44 (0) 20 7584 1363

BoBo Design
T. +44 (0) 1273 400732
www.bobodesign.co.uk

Brinkworth
T. +44 (0) 20 7613 5341
www.brinkworth.co.uk

Bushe Associates
T. +44 (0) 20 7697 0707
www.busheassoc.com

Cardio UK
T. +44 (0) 20 8500 5035
www.cardiouk.com

Christopher Wray Lighting
T. +44 (0) 20 7751 8701
www.christopherwray.com

Connections in Design
T. +44 (0) 121 451 1201
www.connectionsindesign.co.uk

Crescent Lighting
T. +44 (0) 1635 878888
www.crescent.co.uk

Dark
T. +32 050 7181 40
www.dark.be

David Wilds Patton
Lighting Design
T. +1 650 574 2371
www.dwplightingdesign.com

De Marchis Sergison
T. +44 (0) 7810 20+4496

Diffuse
T. +44 (0) 1462 638331
www.diffuse.co.uk

Doug Harper Furniture
T. +44 (0) 20 7837 7876

Ennemlaghi
T. +44 (0) 20 7987 3946

Erco
T. +49 2351 551 100
www.erco.com

Eurolounge
T. +44 (0) 20 7792 5499
www.eurolounge.co.uk

Eva Jiricna Architects
T. +44 (0) 20 7554 2400
www.ejal.com

Focus Lighting Inc.
T. +1 212 865 1565
www.focuslighting.com

Franklite
T. +44 (0) 1908 691818
www.franklite.org

Fulcrum Consulting
T. +44 (0) 20 7520 1300
www.fulcrumfirst.com

Genesis 1:3
T. +44 (0) 20 8845 8444
www.genesis13.com

Georgia Scott Designs
T. +44 (0) 20 7987 0199
www.georgiascott.com

Global Glass Art
T. +44 (0) 20 7419 2202

Greenapple Systems
T. +44 (0) 1727 872525
www.greenapple.co.uk

Inflate
T. +44 (0) 20 7713 9096
www.inflate.co.uk

Integrated Intelligence
T. +44 (0) 20 8768 5195
www.i2automation.net

Isometrix Lighting + Design
T. +44 (0) 20 7253 2888
www.isometrix.co.uk

Kaplan Partners Architectural
Lighting
T. +1 310 552 2191
www.kpal.net

kiki UK
T. +44 (0) 1273 695377
www.kikiuk.com

Lauren Moriarty
T. +44 (0) 7787 562533
www.laurenmoriarty.co.uk

Lighting Research Center
T. +1 518 687 7100
www.lrc.rpi.edu

Ligne Roset
www.ligne-roset.com

Littmann Goddard Hogarth
T. +44 (0) 20 7351 7871
www.lgh-architects.co.uk

Luceplan
T. +39 02 66 24 21
www.luceplan.com

Lutron
T. +44 (0) 207 702 0657
www.lutron.com

Mark Humphrey
T. +44 (0) 20 7348 7500
www.markhumphrey.co.uk

Mathmos
T. +44 (0) 20 7549 2759
www.mathmos.co.uk

Mocha
T. +44 (0) 20 8202 9755
www.mocha-int.com

Modular Lighting Instruments
T. +32 (0) 51 26 56 56
www.supermodular.com

Moooi
T. +31 (0) 76 57 22 070
www.moooi.com

Nelson
T. +44 (0) 20 7627 3375

Optelma
T. +44 (0) 1235 553 769
www.optelma.co.uk

Randall Whitehead
T. +1 415 626 1277
www.randallwhitehead.com

Rare Basics
T. +44 (0) 208 348 9888

Sharon Marston
T. +44 (0) 20 8691 8881
www.sharonmarston.com

SHH Architects
T. +44 (0) 1297 444179

Studio Lux
T. +1 206 284 3417
www.studiolux.com

Sottini
T. +44 (0) 1482 449 513
www.sottini.co.uk

Splinter
T. +44 (0) 151 709 9055
www.splinter.co.uk

Suck UK
T. +44 (0) 20 7923 0011
www.suck.uk.com

Swarovski
T. +44 (0) 20 7016 6780
www.swarovski.com

The Bradley Collection
T. +44 (0) 1449 722724
www.bradleycollection.co.uk

The Colour Light Co
T. +44 (0) 1730 810 942
www.colourlight.com

The Light Lab
T. +44 (0) 20 7278 2678
www.thelightlab.co.uk

Tord Boontje
T. +44 (0) 20 7277 8394
www.transglass.co.uk

Tom Kirk
T. +44 (0) 20 7780 9288
www.tomkirk.com

Tom Dixon
T. +44 (0) 20 7792 5335
www.tomdixon.net

Totem Design
T. +44 (0) 20 7243 0692
www.totem-uk.com

WaveDecor
www.wavedecor.com

Acknowledgements

The driving force behind this book was to produce a visually captivating, inspirational, and practical guide to what can be achieved when we turn our attention to domestic lighting. That has been possible only with the help, support, and encouragement from a whole host of people. Thanks are due.

Firstly, of course, I have to pay a debt of gratitude to all those who contributed to the book, furnishing me with information, stunning visuals, and incisive commentary. With a more design-aware clientele calling on the services of lighting specialists to transform interior and exterior environments, lighting designers and manufacturers are busy folk. But they had the foresight to see just how valuable a book of this nature would be and, with the cream of the lighting crop signed up and on board, the vision for this book has become a reality.

Bright Ideas is very much the result of a team effort and so I thank my publishers, RotoVision. Designer Keith Stephenson and art director Luke Herriott have worked wonders with the look and feel of this book. And my editor, Leonie Taylor, has been very much more than someone who made sure that all the 't's' are crossed and 'i's' dotted. Her guidance and support have been invaluable.

My commitment to this book has meant long hours and an often hermit-like existence. But knowing I've had such great personal support, love, and encouragement has made it all worthwhile. Big thanks, then, to my family—Mum, Dad, Barry, and Darren—all my friends, and my partner's family. Lastly, and most importantly, my biggest thanks go to the love and light of my life, my partner Chris. He's my rock in everything I do and has been behind me 100 percent with his infectious positivity and enthusiasm.

Credits from page 46–47

RED
Lighting
Design Focus Lighting
Location Morimoto Restaurant, Philadelphia
Year 2002
Architect Karim Rashid
Photography David Joseph

ORANGE
Designer Kate Beard
Location Private residence, bedroom
Year 2002
Lighting Colourwash from Isometrix Lighting + Design

YELLOW
Designer Bruce Munro
Year 2000
Dimensions H 150cm (58.5in), W 85cm (33.15in)
Materials Coral Stone

GREEN
Location Bathroom and Lower Living Area, private residence, London, UK
Year 2002
Lighting Colourwash from Isometrix Lighting + Design

BLUE
Designer Bruce Munro
Year 2001
Dimensions (bowl only) H 17cm (6.63in), W 56cm (21.84in)
Material Lead crystal

INDIGO
Designer Bruce Oldfield & Connections in Design
Year 2000
Location Show home, London, UK
Photography Paul Grundy

VIOLET
Designer The Colour Light Company
Year 2001
Location BBC boardroom, London, UK

Credits for pages 2–3 and 4–5

Lighting Erco
Architect Ken Shuttleworth
Year 1998
Location Crescent House, Wiltshire, UK
Photography Frieder Blickle

Credits for Chapter openings

CHAPTER 1
Designer Randall Whitehead
Interior Designer Helen C Reuter
Year 2003
Location Palm Springs, California, USA
Photography Dennis Anderson

CHAPTER 2
Designer Arc Lighting
Year 2001
Dimensions H 15cm^2 (5.85in^2)
Materials Glass
Photography Holly Jolliffe

CHAPTER 3
Designer Randall Whitehead
Interior Designer Helen C Reuter
Year 2003
Location Palm Springs, California
Photography Dennis Anderson

CHAPTER 4
Designer Stefano Giovannoni for Alessi
Year 1999
Dimensions H 15.8cm (6.16in), Diam 11.6cm (4.52in)
Materials Thermoplastic resin

CHAPTER 5
Designer Helena Poch for Taller Uno (distributed by Optelma)
Dimensions L 30cm (11.7in), H 15cm (5.85in)/ L 45cm (17.55in), H 23cm (8.97in)
Materials Wood, linen

Designer Verner Panton
Year 1970
Photography Jefferson Smith

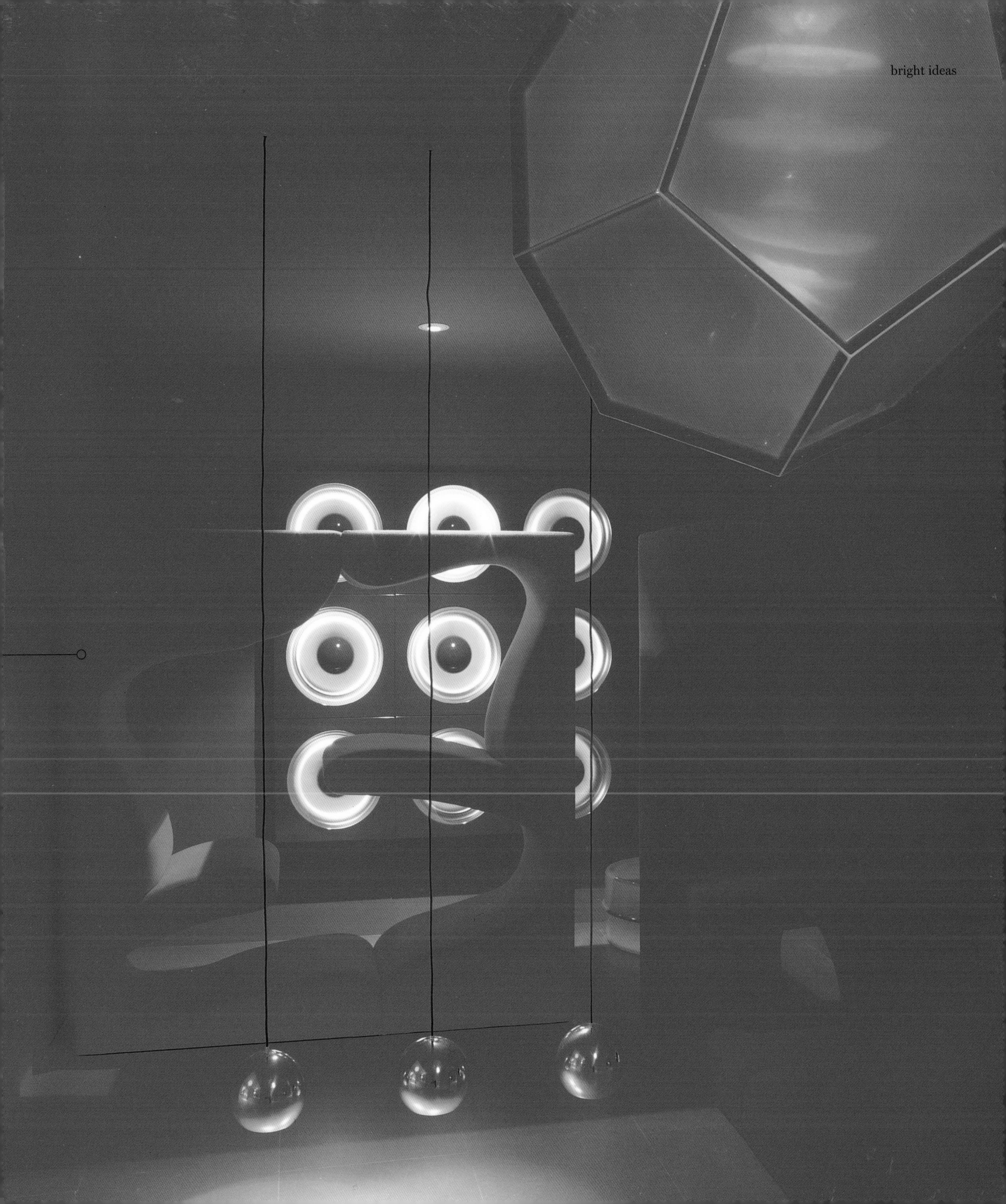